# INSIDE GUIDES

# POISONOUS ANIMALS

Written by
THERESA GREENAWAY

## DORLING KINDERSLEY
London • New York • Stuttgart • Moscow • Sydney

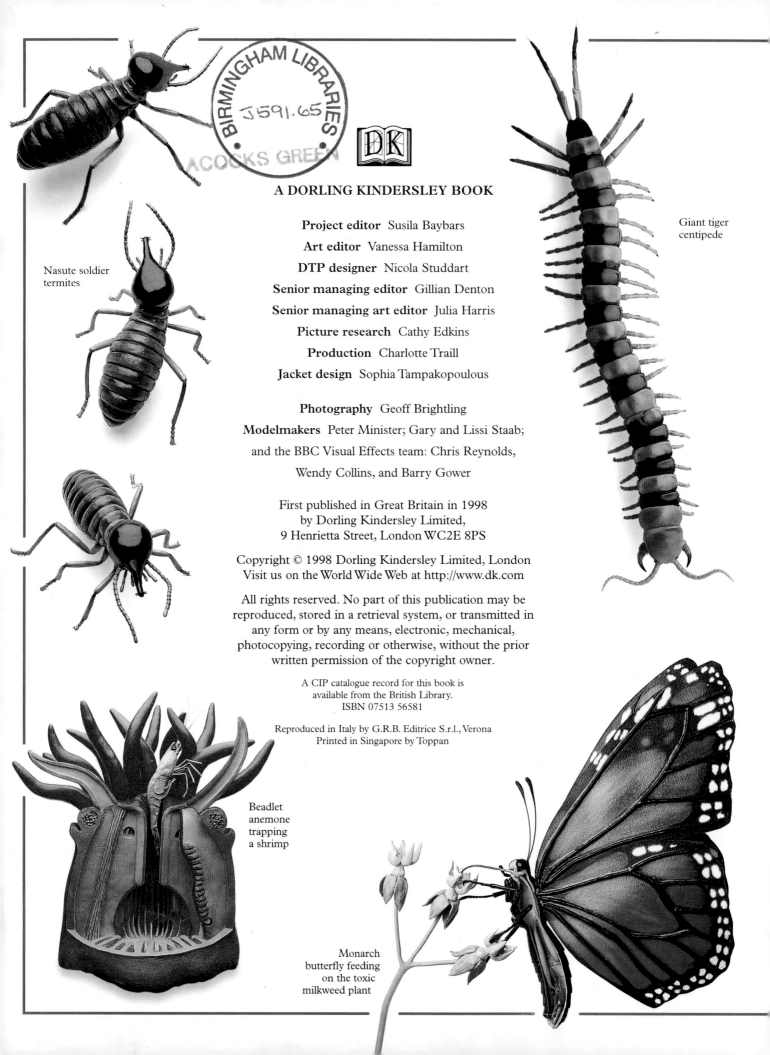

**DK**

# A DORLING KINDERSLEY BOOK

**Project editor**  Susila Baybars
**Art editor**  Vanessa Hamilton
**DTP designer**  Nicola Studdart
**Senior managing editor**  Gillian Denton
**Senior managing art editor**  Julia Harris
**Picture research**  Cathy Edkins
**Production**  Charlotte Traill
**Jacket design**  Sophia Tampakopoulous

**Photography**  Geoff Brightling
**Modelmakers**  Peter Minister; Gary and Lissi Staab;
and the BBC Visual Effects team: Chris Reynolds,
Wendy Collins, and Barry Gower

First published in Great Britain in 1998
by Dorling Kindersley Limited,
9 Henrietta Street, London WC2E 8PS

A CIP catalogue record for this book is
available from the British Library.
ISBN 07513 56581

Reproduced in Italy by G.R.B. Editrice S.r.l., Verona
Printed in Singapore by Toppan

Giant tiger
centipede

Nasute soldier
termites

Beadlet
anemone
trapping
a shrimp

Monarch
butterfly feeding
on the toxic
milkweed plant

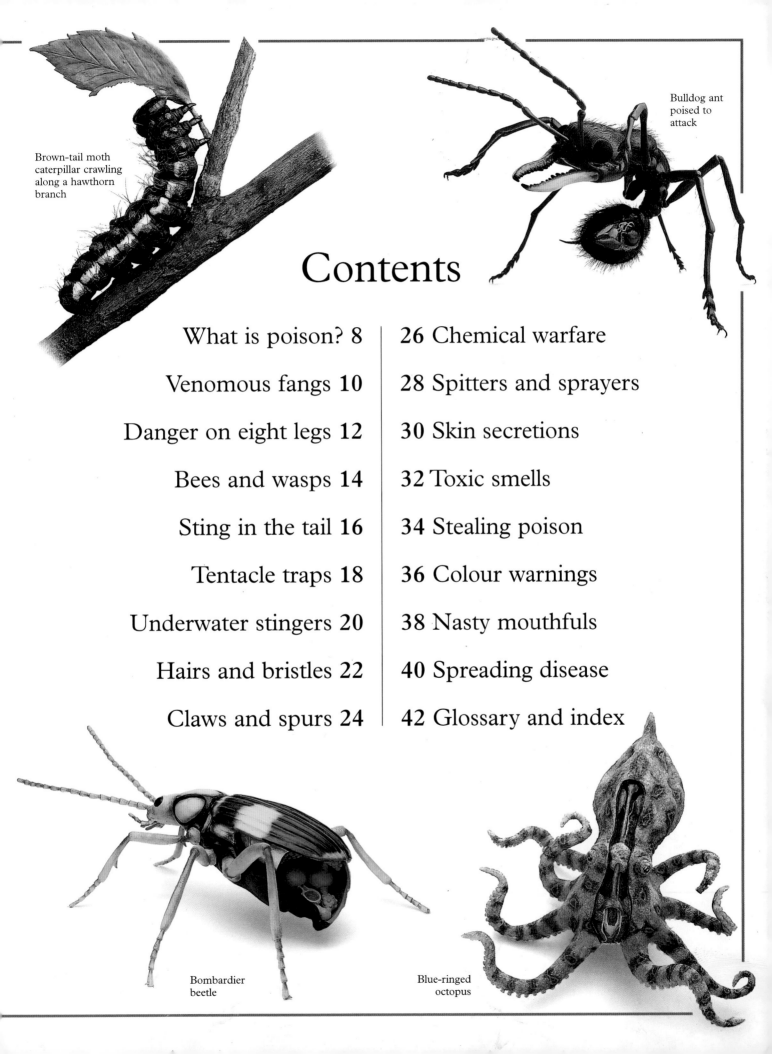

Brown-tail moth caterpillar crawling along a hawthorn branch

Bulldog ant poised to attack

# Contents

Bombardier beetle

Blue-ringed octopus

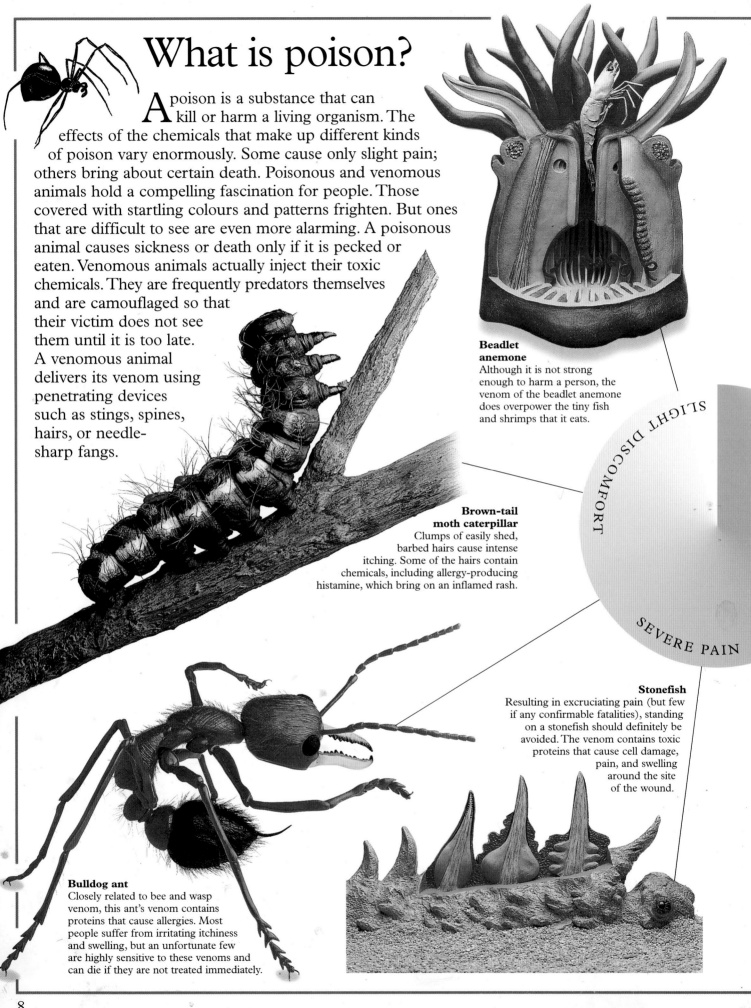

# What is poison?

A poison is a substance that can kill or harm a living organism. The effects of the chemicals that make up different kinds of poison vary enormously. Some cause only slight pain; others bring about certain death. Poisonous and venomous animals hold a compelling fascination for people. Those covered with startling colours and patterns frighten. But ones that are difficult to see are even more alarming. A poisonous animal causes sickness or death only if it is pecked or eaten. Venomous animals actually inject their toxic chemicals. They are frequently predators themselves and are camouflaged so that their victim does not see them until it is too late. A venomous animal delivers its venom using penetrating devices such as stings, spines, hairs, or needle-sharp fangs.

**Beadlet anemone**
Although it is not strong enough to harm a person, the venom of the beadlet anemone does overpower the tiny fish and shrimps that it eats.

**Brown-tail moth caterpillar**
Clumps of easily shed, barbed hairs cause intense itching. Some of the hairs contain chemicals, including allergy-producing histamine, which bring on an inflamed rash.

SLIGHT DISCOMFORT

SEVERE PAIN

**Stonefish**
Resulting in excruciating pain (but few if any confirmable fatalities), standing on a stonefish should definitely be avoided. The venom contains toxic proteins that cause cell damage, pain, and swelling around the site of the wound.

**Bulldog ant**
Closely related to bee and wasp venom, this ant's venom contains proteins that cause allergies. Most people suffer from irritating itchiness and swelling, but an unfortunate few are highly sensitive to these venoms and can die if they are not treated immediately.

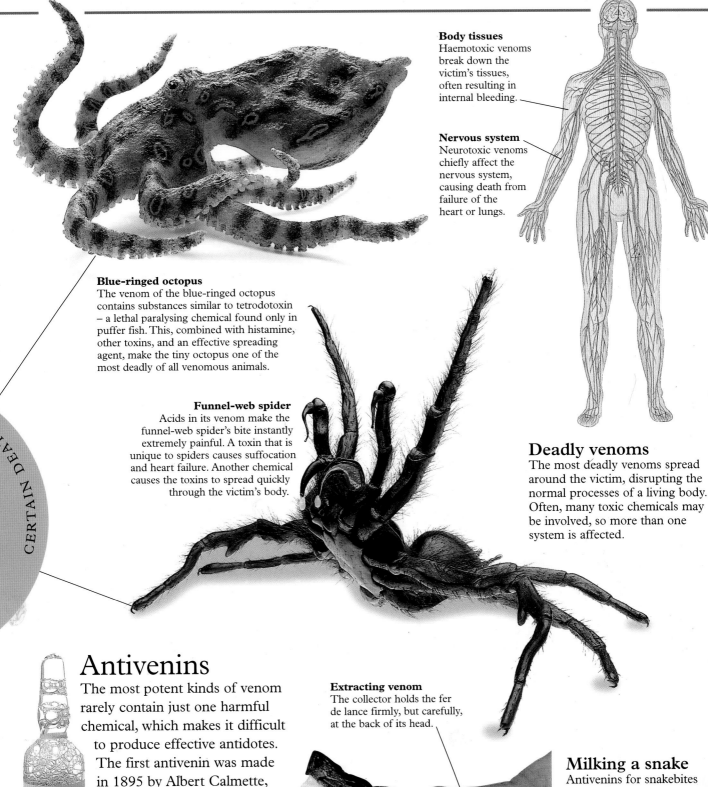

## Body tissues
Haemotoxic venoms break down the victim's tissues, often resulting in internal bleeding.

## Nervous system
Neurotoxic venoms chiefly affect the nervous system, causing death from failure of the heart or lungs.

### Blue-ringed octopus
The venom of the blue-ringed octopus contains substances similar to tetrodotoxin – a lethal paralysing chemical found only in puffer fish. This, combined with histamine, other toxins, and an effective spreading agent, make the tiny octopus one of the most deadly of all venomous animals.

### Funnel-web spider
Acids in its venom make the funnel-web spider's bite instantly extremely painful. A toxin that is unique to spiders causes suffocation and heart failure. Another chemical causes the toxins to spread quickly through the victim's body.

## Deadly venoms
The most deadly venoms spread around the victim, disrupting the normal processes of a living body. Often, many toxic chemicals may be involved, so more than one system is affected.

# Antivenins
The most potent kinds of venom rarely contain just one harmful chemical, which makes it difficult to produce effective antidotes. The first antivenin was made in 1895 by Albert Calmette, a French bacteriologist. Since then, many antivenins have been produced to counter the effects of dangerous snake, spider, and scorpion venoms.

### Extracting venom
The collector holds the fer de lance firmly, but carefully, at the back of its head.

**S ANTIVENOM** 10ml
(RNATUS)
3% Cresol
H/1965)
ee package insert
Do Not Freeze
EXP:
APRIL 1997
for Medical Research
ple, Transvaal
DRINGHAM, 2131

### Antivenin serum
An ampoule of antivenin serum is an important part of a first-aid kit.

## Milking a snake
Antivenins for snakebites are made by "milking" the venom from the snake. It takes many snakes to produce one teaspoon of liquid venom, which is then purified and freeze-dried. Dilute amounts of this are then injected into horses, which are bled regularly to yield a serum. This is used as an antidote to a snakebite from the type that was milked.

# Venomous fangs

Without exception, all snakes are carnivores. Because they are limbless, they cannot hold down their prey. Instead, many snakes possess powerful venoms that quickly paralyse or kill their victims. A snake is able to go without food for a long time. When it does catch a meal, it must swallow it whole, and it has specially adapted jaws to do this. By paralysing or killing its prey first, the snake is able to undertake the lengthy process of swallowing the victim at leisure, without being injured in the process. Snake venom is modified saliva. It is stored in glands and injected into a wound made by the snake's fangs. The venom is an effective defence against large animals, but most snakes do not have venom that is powerful enough to kill a person.

### Sea snake
Sea snakes have left the land and live almost entirely at sea, although some species lay their eggs on shore. The olive sea snake lives in and around coral reefs, where it preys on fish. Sea snakes have some of the most toxic venoms, but fortunately these snakes are not generally aggressive, and rarely bite people.

**Venom gland**
A large venom gland lies on each side of the upper jaw.

**Heat-sensitive pit**
The snake can tell when a warm-blooded animal is close because the heat from its body is picked up by sensitive pits.

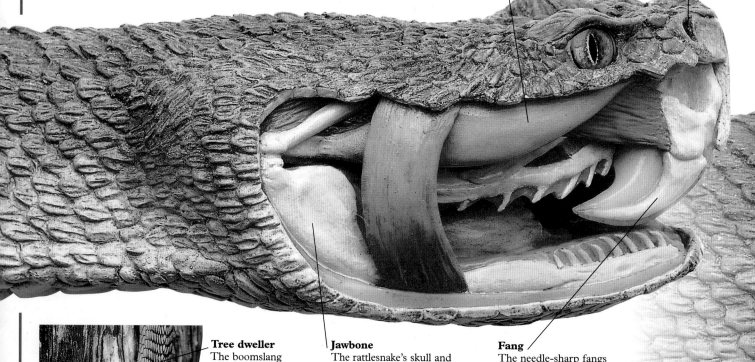

**Tree dweller**
The boomslang snake lives in trees and is common in parts of Africa.

**Jawbone**
The rattlesnake's skull and jawbones are loosely attached to each other, so it can open its mouth very wide.

**Fang**
The needle-sharp fangs are neatly folded away when the snake has its mouth closed and the muscles are relaxed.

### Back-fanged snake
Most back-fanged snakes feed on lizards, birds, or rodents. Their venom is produced in glands connected to enlarged back fangs. For this reason, the snake has to work any prey well into its mouth so that it can chew on it with these teeth. Venom flows down the grooved fangs into the wound. If it manages to get a good grip on a person, a bite from the boomslang may prove fatal. It has a potent venom that causes internal bleeding, often resulting in death.

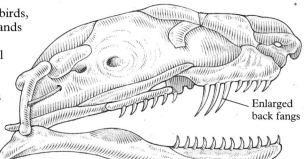

Enlarged back fangs

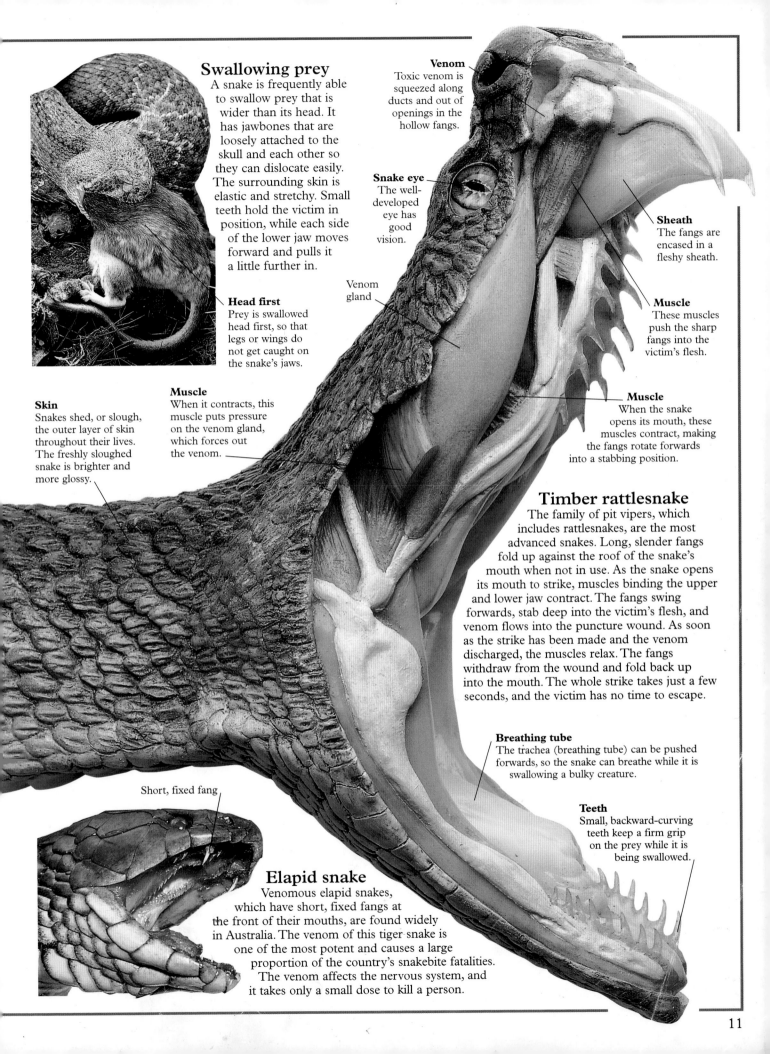

## Swallowing prey

A snake is frequently able to swallow prey that is wider than its head. It has jawbones that are loosely attached to the skull and each other so they can dislocate easily. The surrounding skin is elastic and stretchy. Small teeth hold the victim in position, while each side of the lower jaw moves forward and pulls it a little further in.

**Head first**
Prey is swallowed head first, so that legs or wings do not get caught on the snake's jaws.

**Skin**
Snakes shed, or slough, the outer layer of skin throughout their lives. The freshly sloughed snake is brighter and more glossy.

**Muscle**
When it contracts, this muscle puts pressure on the venom gland, which forces out the venom.

**Venom**
Toxic venom is squeezed along ducts and out of openings in the hollow fangs.

**Snake eye**
The well-developed eye has good vision.

Venom gland

**Sheath**
The fangs are encased in a fleshy sheath.

**Muscle**
These muscles push the sharp fangs into the victim's flesh.

**Muscle**
When the snake opens its mouth, these muscles contract, making the fangs rotate forwards into a stabbing position.

## Timber rattlesnake

The family of pit vipers, which includes rattlesnakes, are the most advanced snakes. Long, slender fangs fold up against the roof of the snake's mouth when not in use. As the snake opens its mouth to strike, muscles binding the upper and lower jaw contract. The fangs swing forwards, stab deep into the victim's flesh, and venom flows into the puncture wound. As soon as the strike has been made and the venom discharged, the muscles relax. The fangs withdraw from the wound and fold back up into the mouth. The whole strike takes just a few seconds, and the victim has no time to escape.

**Breathing tube**
The trachea (breathing tube) can be pushed forwards, so the snake can breathe while it is swallowing a bulky creature.

**Teeth**
Small, backward-curving teeth keep a firm grip on the prey while it is being swallowed.

Short, fixed fang

## Elapid snake

Venomous elapid snakes, which have short, fixed fangs at the front of their mouths, are found widely in Australia. The venom of this tiger snake is one of the most potent and causes a large proportion of the country's snakebite fatalities. The venom affects the nervous system, and it takes only a small dose to kill a person.

# Danger on eight legs

The appearance of a house spider in the sink is enough to strike fear into many people. This extreme terror, or arachnophobia, is really not justified. Most species of spider are in fact quite harmless, and help gardeners and farmers get rid of many insect pests. However, there are a few more sinister spiders that possess venom powerful enough to cause fatalities. The venom is produced in glands located in, or just behind, the spider's fangs, and it is injected as the spider bites. In most cases, soft-bodied spiders use their venom to subdue larger prey that may pose a physical threat to them. Just why spiders like the black widow have venom that is toxic enough to kill a person is a mystery.

**Huge span**
This large spider has a leg span of 12 cm (4.7 in).

**Wandering spider**
Most kinds of spider will try to hide from people, but the Brazilian wandering spider launches an aggressive attack. It is an active hunter whose chief prey is large insects. It has fast-acting venom that causes severe pain to humans and may occasionally result in death.

**Raised forelegs**
A threatened spider rears up and raises its front legs to make itself appear larger and more alarming than it really is.

**Pedipalp**
The tips of a male spider's pedipalps collect sperm and transfer it to the female.

**Making an ambush**
The purse-web spider extends the silk lining of its burrow along the surface of the ground.

**Insect alert**
Vibrations in the silk alert the spider to the presence of an insect.

**Caught!**
Saw-like teeth at the base of the spider's jaws cut the silk so that it can pull its prey into the purse.

**Paralysed prey**
Venom from the long fangs quickly paralyses the prey.

## Caught in a purse
After setting an ambush, the purse-web spider lies in wait in its underground burrow. When an insect walks onto the purse-like trap, the spider acts quickly to pierce the victim's body with its fangs. It drags the paralysed prey down into the burrow and mends the hole before settling down to feed.

## Woodlouse spider
As its name suggests, this spider preys largely on woodlice. Its fangs are strong enough to penetrate their tough armour and can easily pierce a human's skin. Although the spider's venom is not potent enough to kill a person, a severe bite may cause local swelling, and the victim might feel dizzy for a while.

**Attacking the woodlouse**
The spider twists its body so that one fang stabs the soft underside, while the other pierces the back.

## Violin spider

This American spider is one of the most dangerous species of recluse spider. People are usually bitten by violin spiders hiding in clothing or household items. Their venom initially affects only the tissues around the site of the bite. But the black spot that this makes can develop into a huge, slow-healing ulcer, measuring up to 15 cm (6 in) across.

**Natural mark**
A violin-shaped mark on its head gives the spider its name.

**Eye**
The eyes are small and beady.

**Abdomen**
The abdomen contains most of the gut, the heart, the reproductive organs, and the silk-producing organs.

**Furry body**
Hairs on the legs and body are sensitive to touch and help protect the spider.

**Threat position**
The funnel-web rears up to strike because its fangs can only stab downwards.

**Muscle**
Muscle fibres around the venom gland contract to squeeze the venom along ducts in the fangs.

**Fang**
The spider's fangs measure around 7 mm (0.3 in) long.

**Venom**
When the spider is about to strike, venom drips from an opening in the front of the fang.

**Venom gland**
A mixture of acids, enzymes, and powerful nerve poisons are made in the venom glands.

## Funnel-web spider

The Sydney funnel-web is Australia's most infamous spider. The male causes most of the bites as it encounters people in its search for a mate. It measures up to 7 cm (2.8 in) and has fangs that are powerful enough to pierce a human fingernail. The bite of the funnel-web is deep and painful. The venom is highly acidic and contains nerve poisons that paralyse the muscles within minutes. The victim may also suffer sickness, stomach pain, and breathing difficulties.

**Spur**
Males have spurs on their front legs to grip the female while mating.

**Leg**
Three of its four pairs of legs remain on the ground to give the spider a firm base from which to strike.

# Bees and wasps

Social insects, such as honeybees and wasps, live in large colonies in which the larvae (developing young) are dependant on workers for food and protection. Honeybees feed on pollen and nectar from flowers, so they use their stings purely in defence. Wasps feed their young on flesh and use their sting to subdue insect prey. Most people are not in danger from the sting of a single bee or wasp because only a tiny amount of venom is injected. The venom makes an itchy swelling at the site of the sting, but this usually goes away in a day or two. Unfortunately, some people are allergic to substances in the venom and just one sting can cause severe breathing difficulties.

**Eye**
This is made up of many lenses.

**Stripes**
The stripes warn other creatures that bees can be dangerous.

**Abdomen**
The venom apparatus is located in the tip of the bee's abdomen.

**Wing span**
This can measure up to 10 cm (3.9 in).

**Guts**
Digestive organs lie above the sting and venom apparatus.

**Pulling it out**
As the bee flies away, some of its insides are ripped out.

## Solitary wasps

The female tarantula hawk, the world's largest wasp, preys on tarantula spiders. She uses her sting to inject a venom that paralyses, but does not kill, her prey. Secure in a burrow, the wasp then lays a single egg upon the paralysed spider. When it hatches, the wasp grub has a tasty meal.

## 1 Inside a bee

The venom apparatus of a bee is contained in a muscle sac. The sting itself is made up of two barbed darts that are held in a sheath by a pair of guides; together these extend up into a Y-shaped structure. The venom is made in glands and is stored in a venom sac, ready for use.

**Sting**
Barbed sting can be used only once.

Venom sac

**Dufour's gland**
This gland secretes other substances into the wasp venom.

**Sting shaft**
The darts of a wasp's sting are smooth and barbless.

## Inside a wasp

Only queen and worker wasps have a sting. The sting and venom apparatus is very similar to a bee's, but a wasp's sting is not barbed. This means it can easily be withdrawn from a victim's flesh and can be used again. Unlike a bee, a wasp does not die after it has stung.

## Killer honeybees

African honeybees make a lot of honey, but are very aggressive, so they were taken to Brazil and crossed with a more docile species. The new hybrid escaped into the wild and spread to North America. These "killer bees" attack anyone going near their nest and have caused a number of fatalities.

## Social wasps

Social wasps, such as this European wasp, live with other wasps. The workers feed the larvae on grubs, insects, or dead animal flesh, which they first snip up and chew with their mandibles. They use their stings to kill their prey, as well as in defence.

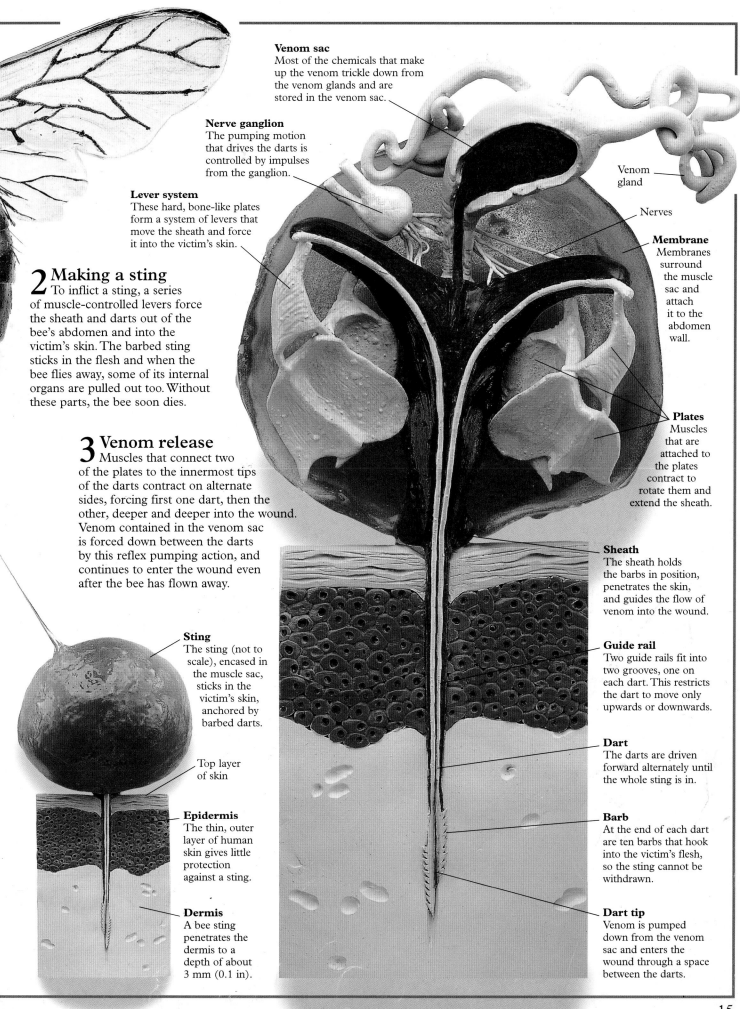

**Venom sac**
Most of the chemicals that make up the venom trickle down from the venom glands and are stored in the venom sac.

**Nerve ganglion**
The pumping motion that drives the darts is controlled by impulses from the ganglion.

**Lever system**
These hard, bone-like plates form a system of levers that move the sheath and force it into the victim's skin.

Venom gland

Nerves

**Membrane**
Membranes surround the muscle sac and attach it to the abdomen wall.

## 2 Making a sting
To inflict a sting, a series of muscle-controlled levers force the sheath and darts out of the bee's abdomen and into the victim's skin. The barbed sting sticks in the flesh and when the bee flies away, some of its internal organs are pulled out too. Without these parts, the bee soon dies.

## 3 Venom release
Muscles that connect two of the plates to the innermost tips of the darts contract on alternate sides, forcing first one dart, then the other, deeper and deeper into the wound. Venom contained in the venom sac is forced down between the darts by this reflex pumping action, and continues to enter the wound even after the bee has flown away.

**Plates**
Muscles that are attached to the plates contract to rotate them and extend the sheath.

**Sheath**
The sheath holds the barbs in position, penetrates the skin, and guides the flow of venom into the wound.

**Guide rail**
Two guide rails fit into two grooves, one on each dart. This restricts the dart to move only upwards or downwards.

**Sting**
The sting (not to scale), encased in the muscle sac, sticks in the victim's skin, anchored by barbed darts.

**Dart**
The darts are driven forward alternately until the whole sting is in.

Top layer of skin

**Barb**
At the end of each dart are ten barbs that hook into the victim's flesh, so the sting cannot be withdrawn.

**Epidermis**
The thin, outer layer of human skin gives little protection against a sting.

**Dermis**
A bee sting penetrates the dermis to a depth of about 3 mm (0.1 in).

**Dart tip**
Venom is pumped down from the venom sac and enters the wound through a space between the darts.

15

# Sting in the tail

Ants and scorpions have formidable jaws that they use to cut up tough insect prey. Jaws this powerful can also deliver a painful nip to larger, soft-skinned animals – and this includes people. Most ants simply spray venom from their rear end into a wound made by their jaws, but a few species actually have a sting to inject their painful venom. All scorpions have a sting and pose a real threat in many tropical countries. A dose of scorpion venom can be fatal, although only around five per cent of all species are considered dangerous to humans. The scorpion's habit of hiding under beds, or in other nooks and crannies, does not endear it to anyone encountering one of them unexpectedly.

**Jointed leg**
All adult insects have three pairs of jointed legs. Long-legged bulldog ants can run very fast.

**Clawed feet**
The ant's feet have tiny hooked claws, which give it a sure grip, no matter what it walks on.

**Trap jaws**
Flexible, toothed jaws can snap around in a semicircle, or wider, to trap prey.

**Springtail**
This primitive jumping insect is the trap-jaw ant's only prey.

**Body**
The ant's narrow-waisted body is very flexible, so it can bend easily to deliver a sting.

**Glandular filament**
Narrow gland filaments are lined with cells that produce venom.

**Midgut**
Food is digested by enzymes in the midgut. The products of digestion are absorbed through the midgut wall.

## Bulldog ant
Australian bulldog ants are large, reaching 3 cm (1.2 in). They live in enormous underground nests and are at their most aggressive if anything disturbs, or comes too close to, their home and young. Serrated mandibles act like pliers to pinch the victim's flesh painfully and firmly. Strong legs steady the ant, allowing it to swing its abdomen into position to insert a wasp-like sting. The smooth, sharp sting can be used again and again.

**Strong stance**
Strong legs steady the ant as it curls its body around and swings its abdomen into position.

## Trap-jaw ant
Not all ants live in huge colonies. The tropical trap-jaw ant inhabits a small nest, concealed in a hollow twig. These tiny ants have elongated jaws that end in interlocking serrations. The jaws are normally bent back, but when the ant detects its springtail prey, they snap forwards to catch it. The ant stings its victim with paralysing venom and carries it back to the nest between its jaws.

**Antenna**
Ants use their highly sensitive antennae to gather information about their surroundings.

**Jaw**
Also called mandibles, the ant's long jaws are efficient tools for gripping food items, as well as enemies.

**Firm grip**
Serrations along the inner edge of its mandibles give the ant extra grip.

**Compound eye**
Large compound eyes enable the ant to detect movement very effectively.

**Gentle giant**
This scorpion stings only if it is stepped on, or if it catches an animal too big to kill with its claws.

Smooth, sharp sting

**Dufour gland**
This gland secretes chemicals that the ant uses to communicate with other ants.

**Venom reservoir**
Venom is stored in a sac-like reservoir.

## Imperial scorpion
This large scorpion preys on small lizards and invertebrates. It grasps its victim with huge claws, then tears it apart with its jaws. The massive pincers and large sting appear truly terrifying to human eyes, but the venom of this species is not a serious threat to people. If stung, a person is likely to suffer more from fright and shock.

**Sting**
The scorpion inserts the tip of its sting into a soft part of its victim's body.

## African fat-tailed scorpion
Native to Tunisia, the fat-tailed scorpion has a deadly venom. It finds houses ideal places to hide and hunt for insects, and is often found lurking in bathrooms. The scorpion's fat tail is powerful, so it can deliver a sting through clothes and even shoes. Without a dose of antivenin, these stings can be fatal.

Sting

**Venom sac**
Muscles around the venom sacs squeeze out the venom in repeated pulses.

**Muscle**
One set of muscles curls the sting back; another set swings it forwards into a stinging position.

## Sting mechanism
The scorpion's tail is segmented and muscular. It can be bent right over the scorpion's head. At the tip of the tail is a swollen, bulb-shaped segment ending in a long, sharp spine. Inside the bulb are two venom sacs. Muscles attached to the base of the bulb move the sting to and fro.

# Tentacle traps

Sea anemones, jellyfish, and corals are simple aquatic animals that all belong to the same group. Common features include a single body opening that both takes in food and passes out waste, and a ring of tentacles around the mouth. They range in size from tiny polyps only 5 mm (0.2 in) long, to the massive lion's mane jellyfish whose bell (body) is over 2 m (6.6 ft) in diameter. All these soft-bodied creatures possess an effective means of self-defence and prey capture – clusters of stinging cells called nematocysts are housed along their tentacles. These microscopic weapons contain a capsule, inside which is a coiled thread and a droplet of venom. When triggered by a contact, thousands of nematocysts inject their venom into the victim's skin.

## Man-of-war

Each large and dangerous Portuguese man-of-war is actually a colony made up of individual animals. One of them forms a gas-filled float and controls buoyancy, some are used for reproduction or feeding, while the others make up the trailing, stinging tentacles. Contact with these tentacles causes immediate sharp pain. Weals take a day or two to go away.

**Trailing tentacles**
The stinging tentacles can be 10 m (32.8 ft) long or more.

## Stinging coral

A coral colony is made up of many tiny polyps, which are armed with nematocysts. The venom from these causes painful, stinging blisters and a breakdown of surface blood vessels, especially if the skin has been broken. In extreme cases, muscles become paralysed.

**Polyp**
Individual polyps make up a coral colony.

**Circular muscle**
This circular band of muscle contracts to close the opening of the pharynx (throat).

## Beadlet anemone

Anchored to rocks in shallow water, this anemone waits for small sea creatures to swim into its outstretched tentacles. As the prey brushes past, thousands of nematocysts fire entangling or stinging threads. The prey gets caught in the tentacles, which bend towards the anemone's mouth and guide the victim into the body cavity.

**Muscle**
Water is expelled when this muscle contracts, reducing the anemone to a jelly-like blob.

**Pedal disc**
This tough, rubbery disc keeps the anemone attached to the rock.

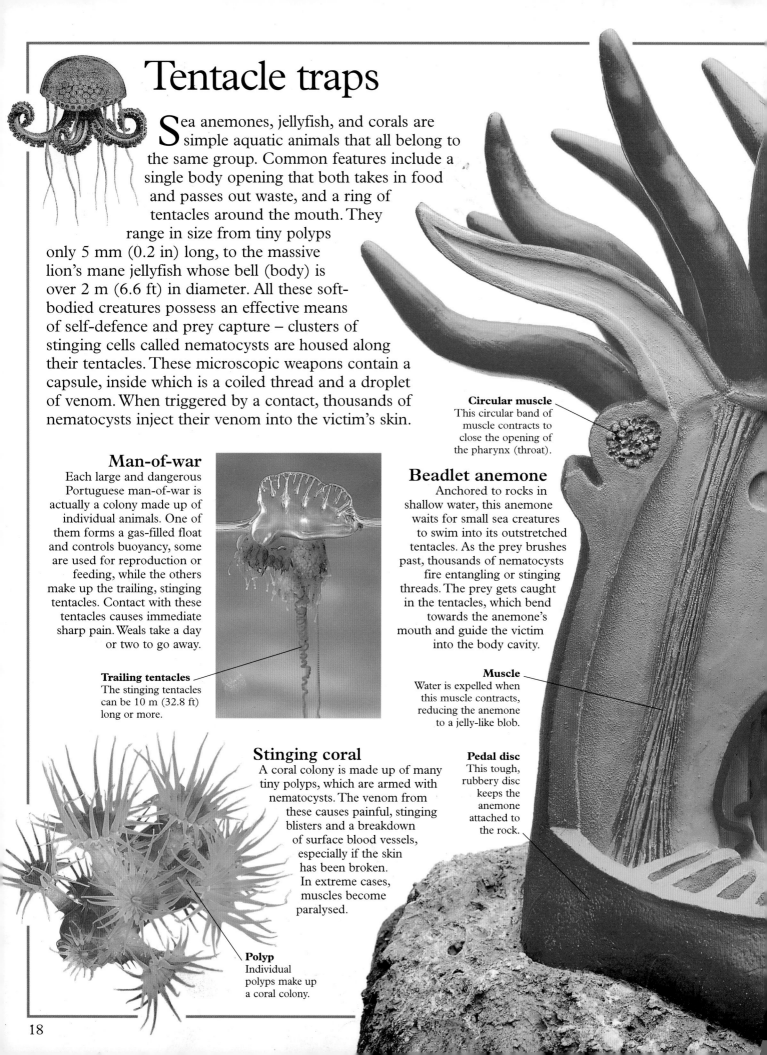

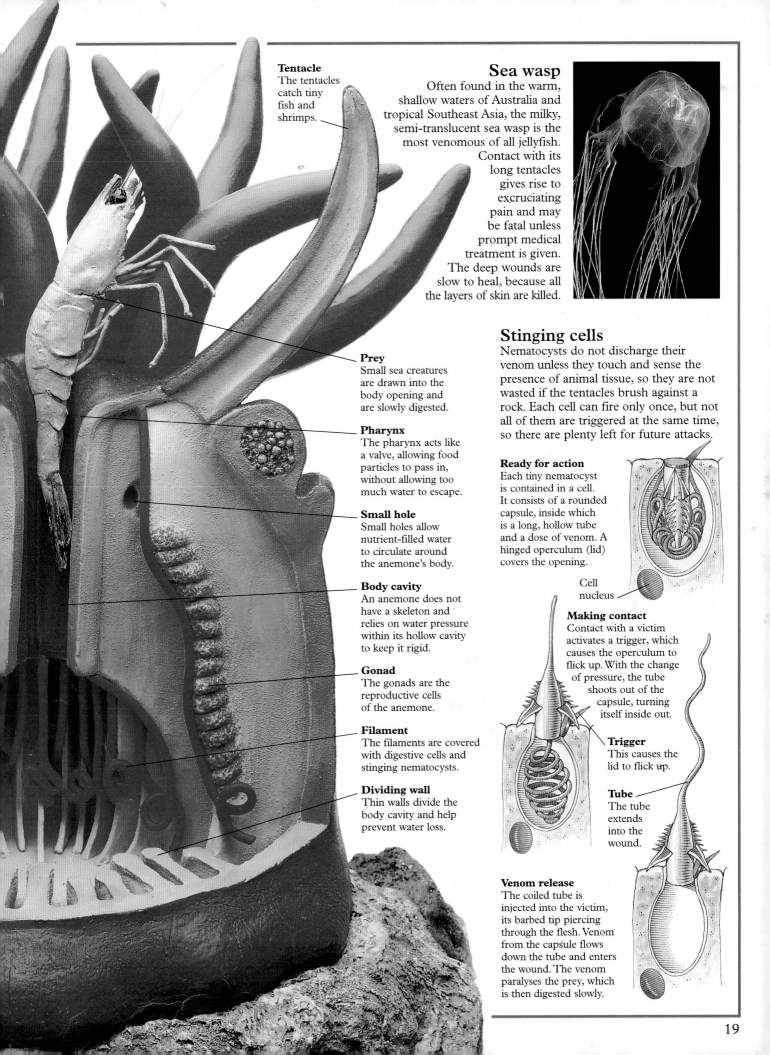

**Tentacle**
The tentacles catch tiny fish and shrimps.

## Sea wasp

Often found in the warm, shallow waters of Australia and tropical Southeast Asia, the milky, semi-translucent sea wasp is the most venomous of all jellyfish. Contact with its long tentacles gives rise to excruciating pain and may be fatal unless prompt medical treatment is given. The deep wounds are slow to heal, because all the layers of skin are killed.

**Prey**
Small sea creatures are drawn into the body opening and are slowly digested.

**Pharynx**
The pharynx acts like a valve, allowing food particles to pass in, without allowing too much water to escape.

**Small hole**
Small holes allow nutrient-filled water to circulate around the anemone's body.

**Body cavity**
An anemone does not have a skeleton and relies on water pressure within its hollow cavity to keep it rigid.

**Gonad**
The gonads are the reproductive cells of the anemone.

**Filament**
The filaments are covered with digestive cells and stinging nematocysts.

**Dividing wall**
Thin walls divide the body cavity and help prevent water loss.

## Stinging cells

Nematocysts do not discharge their venom unless they touch and sense the presence of animal tissue, so they are not wasted if the tentacles brush against a rock. Each cell can fire only once, but not all of them are triggered at the same time, so there are plenty left for future attacks.

**Ready for action**
Each tiny nematocyst is contained in a cell. It consists of a rounded capsule, inside which is a long, hollow tube and a dose of venom. A hinged operculum (lid) covers the opening.

Cell nucleus

**Making contact**
Contact with a victim activates a trigger, which causes the operculum to flick up. With the change of pressure, the tube shoots out of the capsule, turning itself inside out.

**Trigger**
This causes the lid to flick up.

**Tube**
The tube extends into the wound.

**Venom release**
The coiled tube is injected into the victim, its barbed tip piercing through the flesh. Venom from the capsule flows down the tube and enters the wound. The venom paralyses the prey, which is then digested slowly.

# Underwater stingers

The oceans teem with thousands of fish, crustaceans, and other invertebrates, many of which are fierce predators. To avoid being eaten, some marine creatures are equipped with powerful venoms, which are often injected by means of sharp spines. Unfortunately, it is not their natural enemies, but people paddling, swimming, or diving who frequently become the victims of these creatures. Marine venoms are especially potent because fish, unlike humans, are not particularly susceptible to their effects. There is also the risk that unless properly cleaned, wounds made by even minor stings may become infected with bacteria, causing long-lasting ulcers.

**Heel**
The pressure of the victim's heel removes the blockage.

**Blocked tip**
Ducts leading upwards from the venom sacs are blocked at the tip.

**Groove**
Venom travels along ducts that run up two grooves in each spine.

**Venom sac**
There is a pair of venom sacs beside each spine.

**Sharp spine**
The sharp venom spines are coverted with warty skin.

**Small spine**
Ten smaller spines slope backwards.

**Good camouflage**
Textured brown skin makes the stonefish blend in with the sandy seabed.

**1 Venom spine**
Each venomous spine is covered with skin. If someone treads on the stonefish, the sharp tips of the spines stick through the fish's skin and puncture the foot. The spines are tough enough to pierce through even beach shoes.

**2 Venom release**
The pressure of the foot bursts the venom sacs and venom spurts upwards along grooves in the spine and spreads through the puncture wound. The venom release is explosive and can shoot up to 23 cm (9.1 in) into the air.

## Stonefish
A stonefish leads an inactive life, lying buried in the seabed for up to four months at a time. It is one of the most venomous fish in the world, but it uses its potent venom for self-defence rather than capturing prey. The dorsal fin contains 13 venomous spines that the fish raises if it detects a threat.

**Pincer**
When the pincers open, the urchin resembles a clump of tiny flowers.

## Toxic sea urchin
This flower urchin is covered with short non-venomous spines. But between the spines are numerous pedicellariae – stalked structures topped by three tiny, fanged pincers – each of which contains a venom gland. When provoked, the pincers snap shut, biting the adversary and injecting venom into the wound.

**Penetration**
The spine can penetrate a human heel to a depth of 1 cm (0.4 in).

**Destroyed sac**
After discharging, the venom sacs repair themselves and refill.

**Eye**
An alert eye peeks out of the sand.

**3 Venom effect**
The effects of stonefish venom are immediate and severe. An agonising pain develops at the site of the wound and soon spreads to the entire limb, which swells up. Death is rare, but can occur if the wound becomes infected.

## Crown-of-thorns
One of these starfish can measure 30 cm (11.8 in) across. Long, sharp spines cover its upper surface, with shorter, blunter ones below. Each spine is a single sharp crystal, and the longer ones have three cutting edges at their tip. Contact with the crown-of-thorns may result in multiple cuts. Venom is not actively injected, but the starfish's toxic body tissues may infect the wound, causing a severe throbbing pain.

## Stingray
A stingray spends a lot of time lying motionless on the seabed, half covered by silt and sand. If stepped on, its long tail whips upwards in a reflex action, driving a needle-sharp, venomous spine deep into the victim's flesh. The stab wound may penetrate large blood vessels, causing a severe loss of blood.

# Hairs and bristles

Soft-bodied insects and other invertebrates need some means of protecting themselves against the sharp beaks and teeth of larger predators. One way is to have loosely attached hairs and bristles. The hooks on barbed hairs stick to the predator's mouth or tongue, and may pierce the skin, causing pain and irritation. Some release allergy-causing histamines or venoms that cause rashes and swelling. The creatures that possess these stinging hairs often advertise their danger with warning colouring. Unfortunately, many brightly patterned caterpillars, with their gaudy tufts of hair, are attractive to children, who get a nasty rash if they touch or play with them.

**Hawthorn leaf**
The caterpillar's diet consists entirely of leaves.

**Irritant hairs**
The spider's abdomen is covered in loosely attached hairs.

## Head-to-tail
Pine processionary moth caterpillars rest all day in large, communal nests of silk. During the night they feed on pine foliage, travelling head-to-tail along trails marked by the leader. The tufts of brown hair that cover their bodies readily break off if the caterpillars are molested. This acts as a deterrent against birds, but the hairs also irritate human skin, causing rashes.

## Red-kneed tarantula
Although large, this tropical spider is not aggressive and will seldom bite people unless provoked. To protect itself from birds and small mammals, the red-kneed tarantula rubs its abdomen with its hind legs, flicking hundreds of irritating hairs into the face of its assailant.

**Giant anthelid cocoon**
This may be 9 cm (3.5 in) long, or more.

**Hair**
The barbed hairs break in the predator's skin and are difficult to remove.

## Hairy caterpillar
The caterpillar of the brown-tail moth looks pretty, but its colours should be a warning not to touch or get too close. The hairs that grow from tubercles along its soft body are highly irritant, and you don't have to touch the caterpillar to suffer their effects. It sheds its hairs easily, so that just sitting beneath a tree in which some caterpillars are feeding is enough to bring on a rash.

## Prickly cocoon
While a caterpillar is pupating, it is very vulnerable. But caterpillars with poisonous hairs have a good means of defence. As the caterpillar spins itself a cocoon of silk, it moults the hairs into the structure of the cocoon. The hairs stick out all over, and if touched will pierce the skin, causing blisters and itchy rashes.

**Clasper**
A pair of hooked claspers ensure a firm grip on leaves and twigs.

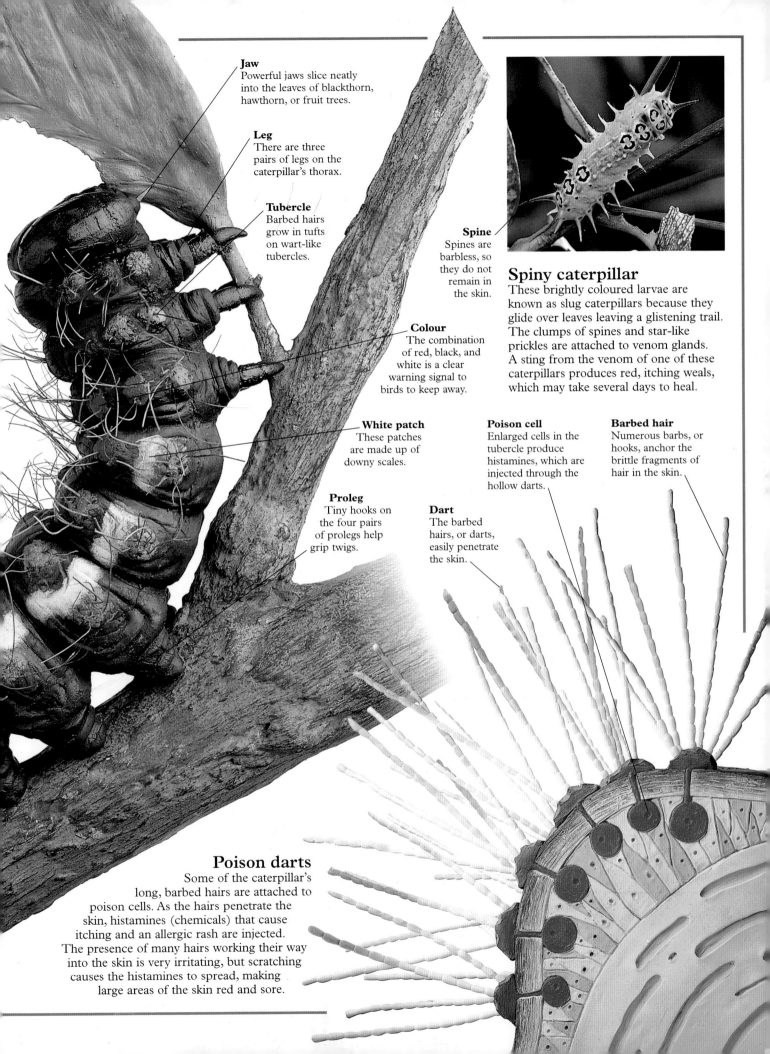

**Jaw**
Powerful jaws slice neatly
into the leaves of blackthorn,
hawthorn, or fruit trees.

**Leg**
There are three
pairs of legs on the
caterpillar's thorax.

**Tubercle**
Barbed hairs
grow in tufts
on wart-like
tubercles.

**Spine**
Spines are
barbless, so
they do not
remain in
the skin.

**Colour**
The combination
of red, black, and
white is a clear
warning signal to
birds to keep away.

**White patch**
These patches
are made up of
downy scales.

**Proleg**
Tiny hooks on
the four pairs
of prolegs help
grip twigs.

## Spiny caterpillar
These brightly coloured larvae are
known as slug caterpillars because they
glide over leaves leaving a glistening trail.
The clumps of spines and star-like
prickles are attached to venom glands.
A sting from the venom of one of these
caterpillars produces red, itching weals,
which may take several days to heal.

**Poison cell**
Enlarged cells in the
tubercle produce
histamines, which are
injected through the
hollow darts.

**Barbed hair**
Numerous barbs, or
hooks, anchor the
brittle fragments of
hair in the skin.

**Dart**
The barbed
hairs, or darts,
easily penetrate
the skin.

## Poison darts
Some of the caterpillar's
long, barbed hairs are attached to
poison cells. As the hairs penetrate the
skin, histamines (chemicals) that cause
itching and an allergic rash are injected.
The presence of many hairs working their way
into the skin is very irritating, but scratching
causes the histamines to spread, making
large areas of the skin red and sore.

# Claws and spurs

An animal uses its claws for many purposes. Frequently very sharp, and sometimes large and tough, claws may be used for digging holes and climbing trees, as well as for self-defence and bringing down prey. Because they are in contact with the soil, claws become contaminated with harmful bacteria. Unless cleaned properly, a scratch from a claw readily becomes infected. Very few animals have venomous claws. Those that do, like many centipedes, have ones that are highly modified, so they do not come in contact with the ground. When not in use, a platypus' claws, or spurs, lie flat against its ankles, in a fleshy sheath.

## Garden centipede

Common, or garden, centipedes are just 3 cm (1.2 in) long. This small centipede relies entirely on vibrations to find its prey. A pinch from its venom claws delivers a dose that paralyses the victim and makes sure it does not escape.

**Small but deadly**
An attack from this centipede has been known to kill a dog.

## Australian centipede

Although not known to cause fatalities, the claws of this 12.5-cm (4.9-in) long centipede from Australia can inject enough venom to make a person feel sick for a week. It causes severe pain and swelling at the site of the wound.

## Tiger centipede

Giant centipedes are found in tropical rainforests worldwide. This one measures up to 24 cm (9.5 in) in length. From above, the huge venom-containing claws look like fearsome fangs. The centipede uses its claws for paralysing prey, as well as for defence.

**Back legs**
Two large legs keep a firm hold on the prey while venom is injected.

**Good swimmer**
The platypus lives mainly in rivers or streams.

## Platypus spur

If the platypus is picked up, it clenches its legs, kicking inwards to plunge two stout spurs deep into its assailant's flesh. A stab from these claws is painful in itself, but in addition, venom is injected into the wound. This causes extremely severe pain, which spreads all over the body.

**Venom gland**
The gland is embedded in the muscles of the platypus' leg.

**Venom duct**
A duct carries the venom down to the ankle and into the base of a hard spur.

**Spur**
The spur pokes through a flap of skin on the inside of the platypus' ankle.

## Platypus

With its short fur and broad, rubbery bill, this primitive egg-laying mammal looks quite harmless. However, it is quite risky to pick up an adult male. A sharp spur on the inside of each hind foot can cause much damage.

**Antenna**
Two jointed antennae help the centipede find its way around and detect food.

**Injecting venom**
The tip of the claw penetrates the victim's body, then venom trickles out of a small opening.

**Duct**
Venom is squeezed down venom ducts into the tip of the venom claw.

**Nerve**
Impulses from the nerves cause the muscles to contract.

**Muscle**
Muscles inside the claw contract to move it towards the other claw in a pinching action.

**Venom gland**
This sac secretes the venom and stores it until it is needed.

**Venom claw**
This highly modified claw has a broad basal section that is large enough to contain the bulky venom gland.

**Leg**
Each body segment has one pair of legs. Tiger centipedes can have up to 23 pairs.

**Walking along**
Many pairs of legs lift the centipede off the ground, so that its body does not catch against leaves or twigs.

**Breathing hole**
A breathing hole, called a spiracle, lies above the leg on each body segement.

**Cuticle**
An outer covering of tough cuticle protects the centipede in its rainforest home.

# Venom claws
Projecting from the underside of its body, the centipede's stout venom claws are spread wide, ready to close on its prey. Once the victim is immobilised by a dose of paralysing venom, the centipede sets to work with its jaws, slicing it into fragments small enough to swallow.

**Colour**
The giant tiger centipede's orange-and-black pattern is a clear warning to anything that gets too close not to venture any nearer.

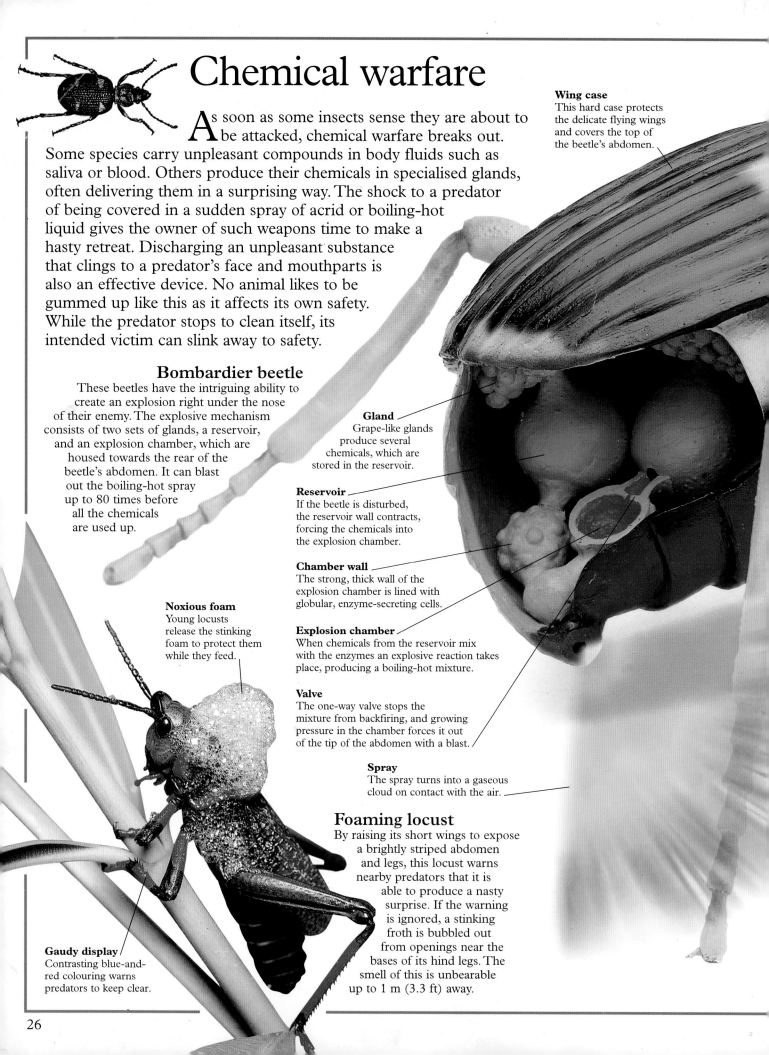

# Chemical warfare

As soon as some insects sense they are about to be attacked, chemical warfare breaks out. Some species carry unpleasant compounds in body fluids such as saliva or blood. Others produce their chemicals in specialised glands, often delivering them in a surprising way. The shock to a predator of being covered in a sudden spray of acrid or boiling-hot liquid gives the owner of such weapons time to make a hasty retreat. Discharging an unpleasant substance that clings to a predator's face and mouthparts is also an effective device. No animal likes to be gummed up like this as it affects its own safety. While the predator stops to clean itself, its intended victim can slink away to safety.

## Bombardier beetle

These beetles have the intriguing ability to create an explosion right under the nose of their enemy. The explosive mechanism consists of two sets of glands, a reservoir, and an explosion chamber, which are housed towards the rear of the beetle's abdomen. It can blast out the boiling-hot spray up to 80 times before all the chemicals are used up.

**Wing case**
This hard case protects the delicate flying wings and covers the top of the beetle's abdomen.

**Gland**
Grape-like glands produce several chemicals, which are stored in the reservoir.

**Reservoir**
If the beetle is disturbed, the reservoir wall contracts, forcing the chemicals into the explosion chamber.

**Chamber wall**
The strong, thick wall of the explosion chamber is lined with globular, enzyme-secreting cells.

**Explosion chamber**
When chemicals from the reservoir mix with the enzymes an explosive reaction takes place, producing a boiling-hot mixture.

**Valve**
The one-way valve stops the mixture from backfiring, and growing pressure in the chamber forces it out of the tip of the abdomen with a blast.

**Spray**
The spray turns into a gaseous cloud on contact with the air.

**Noxious foam**
Young locusts release the stinking foam to protect them while they feed.

## Foaming locust

By raising its short wings to expose a brightly striped abdomen and legs, this locust warns nearby predators that it is able to produce a nasty surprise. If the warning is ignored, a stinking froth is bubbled out from openings near the bases of its hind legs. The smell of this is unbearable up to 1 m (3.3 ft) away.

**Gaudy display**
Contrasting blue-and-red colouring warns predators to keep clear.

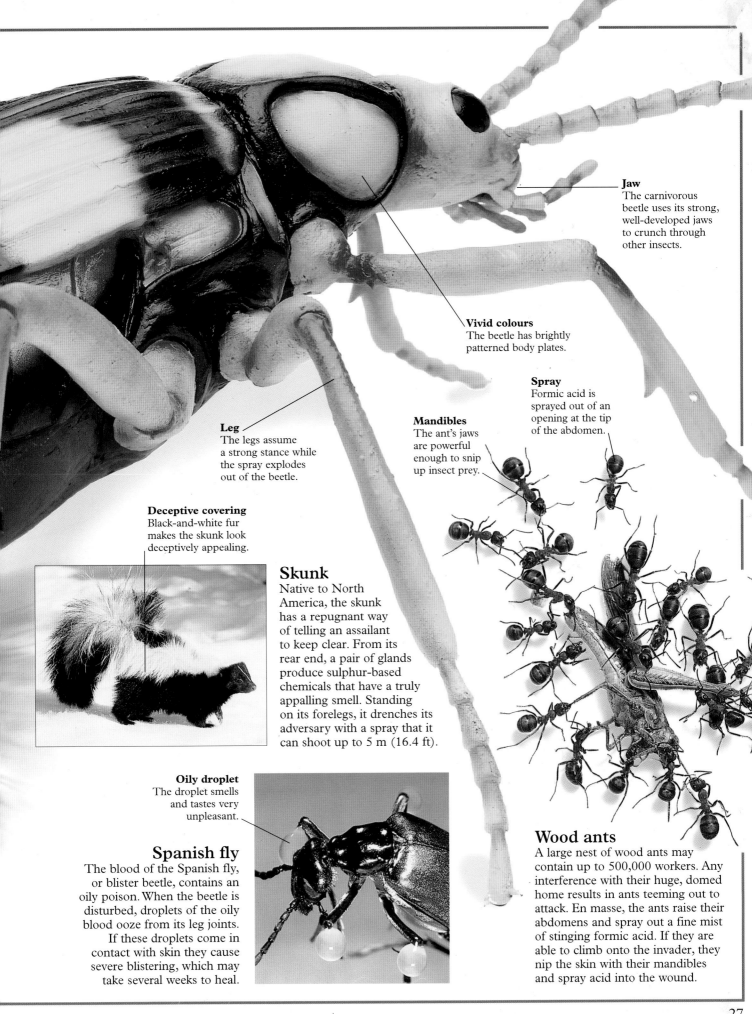

**Jaw**
The carnivorous beetle uses its strong, well-developed jaws to crunch through other insects.

**Vivid colours**
The beetle has brightly patterned body plates.

**Spray**
Formic acid is sprayed out of an opening at the tip of the abdomen.

**Mandibles**
The ant's jaws are powerful enough to snip up insect prey.

**Leg**
The legs assume a strong stance while the spray explodes out of the beetle.

**Deceptive covering**
Black-and-white fur makes the skunk look deceptively appealing.

## Skunk

Native to North America, the skunk has a repugnant way of telling an assailant to keep clear. From its rear end, a pair of glands produce sulphur-based chemicals that have a truly appalling smell. Standing on its forelegs, it drenches its adversary with a spray that it can shoot up to 5 m (16.4 ft).

**Oily droplet**
The droplet smells and tastes very unpleasant.

## Spanish fly

The blood of the Spanish fly, or blister beetle, contains an oily poison. When the beetle is disturbed, droplets of the oily blood ooze from its leg joints. If these droplets come in contact with skin they cause severe blistering, which may take several weeks to heal.

## Wood ants

A large nest of wood ants may contain up to 500,000 workers. Any interference with their huge, domed home results in ants teeming out to attack. En masse, the ants raise their abdomens and spray out a fine mist of stinging formic acid. If they are able to climb onto the invader, they nip the skin with their mandibles and spray acid into the wound.

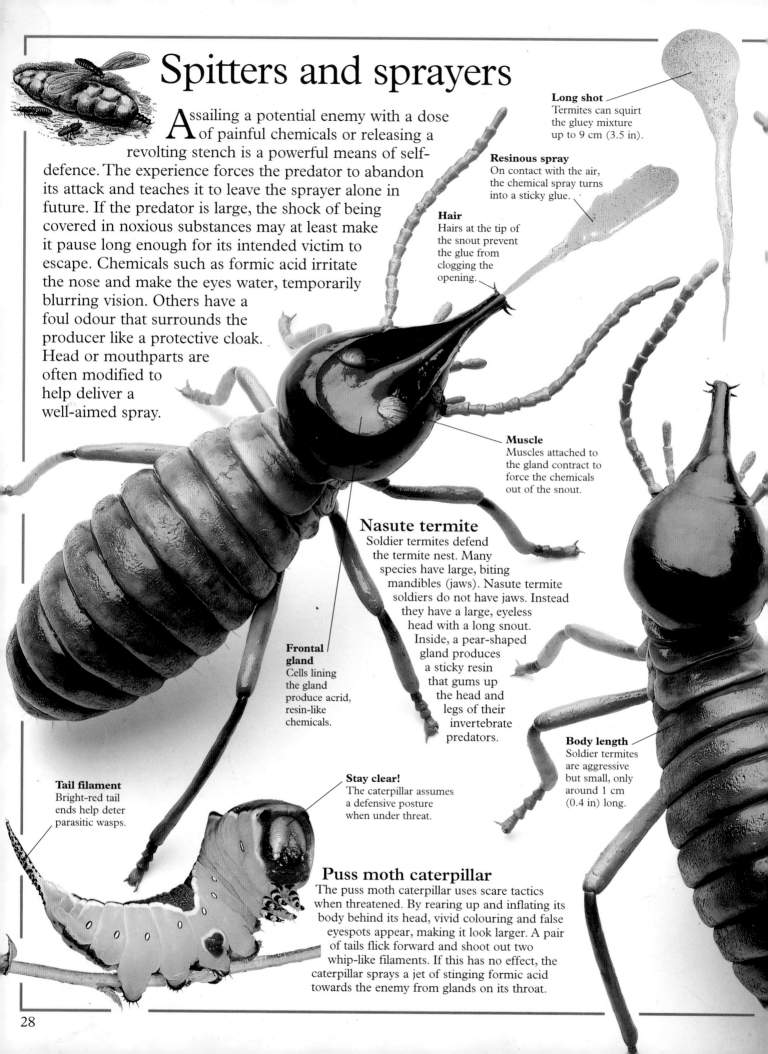

# Spitters and sprayers

Assailing a potential enemy with a dose of painful chemicals or releasing a revolting stench is a powerful means of self-defence. The experience forces the predator to abandon its attack and teaches it to leave the sprayer alone in future. If the predator is large, the shock of being covered in noxious substances may at least make it pause long enough for its intended victim to escape. Chemicals such as formic acid irritate the nose and make the eyes water, temporarily blurring vision. Others have a foul odour that surrounds the producer like a protective cloak. Head or mouthparts are often modified to help deliver a well-aimed spray.

**Long shot**
Termites can squirt the gluey mixture up to 9 cm (3.5 in).

**Resinous spray**
On contact with the air, the chemical spray turns into a sticky glue.

**Hair**
Hairs at the tip of the snout prevent the glue from clogging the opening.

**Muscle**
Muscles attached to the gland contract to force the chemicals out of the snout.

## Nasute termite
Soldier termites defend the termite nest. Many species have large, biting mandibles (jaws). Nasute termite soldiers do not have jaws. Instead they have a large, eyeless head with a long snout. Inside, a pear-shaped gland produces a sticky resin that gums up the head and legs of their invertebrate predators.

**Frontal gland**
Cells lining the gland produce acrid, resin-like chemicals.

**Body length**
Soldier termites are aggressive but small, only around 1 cm (0.4 in) long.

**Tail filament**
Bright-red tail ends help deter parasitic wasps.

**Stay clear!**
The caterpillar assumes a defensive posture when under threat.

## Puss moth caterpillar
The puss moth caterpillar uses scare tactics when threatened. By rearing up and inflating its body behind its head, vivid colouring and false eyespots appear, making it look larger. A pair of tails flick forward and shoot out two whip-like filaments. If this has no effect, the caterpillar sprays a jet of stinging formic acid towards the enemy from glands on its throat.

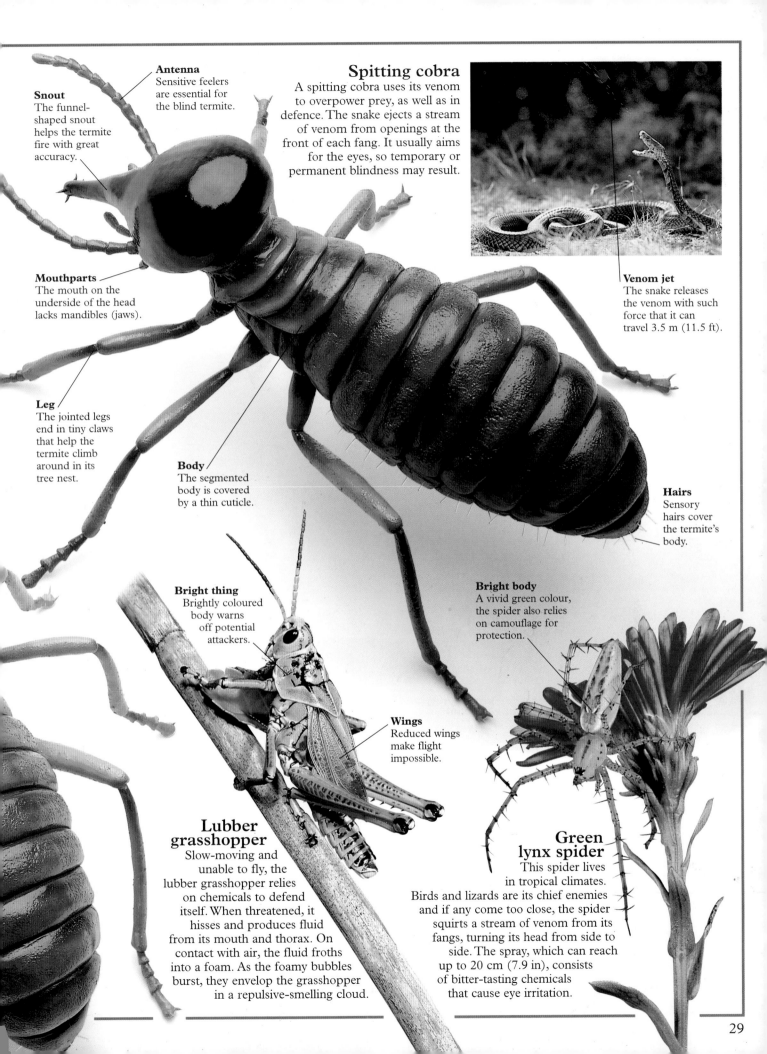

**Snout**
The funnel-shaped snout helps the termite fire with great accuracy.

**Antenna**
Sensitive feelers are essential for the blind termite.

**Mouthparts**
The mouth on the underside of the head lacks mandibles (jaws).

**Leg**
The jointed legs end in tiny claws that help the termite climb around in its tree nest.

**Body**
The segmented body is covered by a thin cuticle.

## Spitting cobra
A spitting cobra uses its venom to overpower prey, as well as in defence. The snake ejects a stream of venom from openings at the front of each fang. It usually aims for the eyes, so temporary or permanent blindness may result.

**Venom jet**
The snake releases the venom with such force that it can travel 3.5 m (11.5 ft).

**Hairs**
Sensory hairs cover the termite's body.

**Bright thing**
Brightly coloured body warns off potential attackers.

**Bright body**
A vivid green colour, the spider also relies on camouflage for protection.

**Wings**
Reduced wings make flight impossible.

## Lubber grasshopper
Slow-moving and unable to fly, the lubber grasshopper relies on chemicals to defend itself. When threatened, it hisses and produces fluid from its mouth and thorax. On contact with air, the fluid froths into a foam. As the foamy bubbles burst, they envelop the grasshopper in a repulsive-smelling cloud.

## Green lynx spider
This spider lives in tropical climates. Birds and lizards are its chief enemies and if any come too close, the spider squirts a stream of venom from its fangs, turning its head from side to side. The spray, which can reach up to 20 cm (7.9 in), consists of bitter-tasting chemicals that cause eye irritation.

# Skin secretions

All predators have to be on their guard and ready to attack at all times. Staying in prime condition is important, because if it is sick or injured a predator cannot hunt for food and may fall prey to another carnivore that feeds on it. For this reason, most predators will not risk injury from something that frightens them, and a potential dinner that suddenly springs an unpleasant surprise on its hungry aggressor has a good chance of getting away. The sudden appearance of unpleasant skin secretions is an effective shock tactic that is widely used by amphibians. Sticky, smelly liquids that cause immediate sickness and vomiting are extremely off-putting. Even people avoid touching animals with slimy skin and will quickly drop a creature that unexpectedly turns wet and smelly in their hands.

**Poison skin**
South American Indians used the frog's toxic skin poisons to tip their hunting darts.

## Poison-dart frogs
Tiny and brilliantly coloured, the poison-dart frogs from South and Central America have highly toxic skin poisons. The poison acts quickly to affect the nerves and muscles. In some cases, just one minute drop of poison is all that is needed to kill an adult person.

**Golden mantella**
The skin of this mantella from Madagascar produces the same kind of chemicals as poison-dart frogs.

## Fire salamander
Short, stocky legs carry this European salamander slowly through damp mountain forests. Birds and mammals that might consider eating it are deterred by the copious amounts of toxic secretions that are produced all over the surface of its skin.

**Variable colouring**
Black body may be patterned with either yellow or orange spots, stripes, or blotches.

## Giant millipede
A red-fronted lemur feeds eagerly on all kinds of crunchy invertebrates, but it has to be careful when dealing with the giant millipede. When attacked, the millipede oozes quantities of poisonous, distasteful liquids onto its black-and-red case. In order to eat it, the lemur first rolls it about in its forepaws, dribbling on it and wiping off the nasty secretions with its tail.

**Parotoid gland**

## California newt
Without their extremely toxic skin secretions, these little newts, just 7.5 cm (3 in) long, would fall prey to many different kinds of birds, reptiles, and mammals. The poison, which is very similar to that of the puffer fish, is present in their internal organs as well as their skin.

**Bright belly**
The newt reveals a bright orange underside in its threat position.

**Eye**
Protruding, bulgy eyes enable the toad to detect movements in a wide field of vision.

**Parotoid gland**
If the gland is squeezed, the poison may squirt out up to 1 m (3.3 ft).

**Poison gland**
Cells lining the wall of the parotoid glands secrete a mixture of different poisons.

**Poison**
The frothy, white cocktail of toxic chemicals affects the function of the heart and muscles.

## Cane toad

The ugly cane toad has a concentrated mass of poison-secreting cells in a swollen patch behind each ear. These are called parotoid glands. If the toad is frightened, toxic milky-white secretions ooze from pores in these glands. Predators, such as cats and dogs, that eat the cane toad may die shortly afterwards, but humans are less severely affected.

**Mouth**
A wide mouth enables the toad to engulf a large invertebrate or a small mammal in one gulp.

**Eardrum**
Toads have no external ear, but the eardrum lies on the surface of its head.

**Parotoid gland**
Each parotoid gland contains a mass of small poison glands embedded in a thick layer of skin.

**Dull colouring**
Unlike most poisonous animals, the cane toad does not warn off its predators with brightly coloured skin tones.

**Toe**
Toads have four toes on their front feet and five on their back.

**Warty skin**
The cane toad can reach a considerable size – up to 23 cm (9.1 in) – but warty, brown skin keeps it well camouflaged.

# Toxic smells

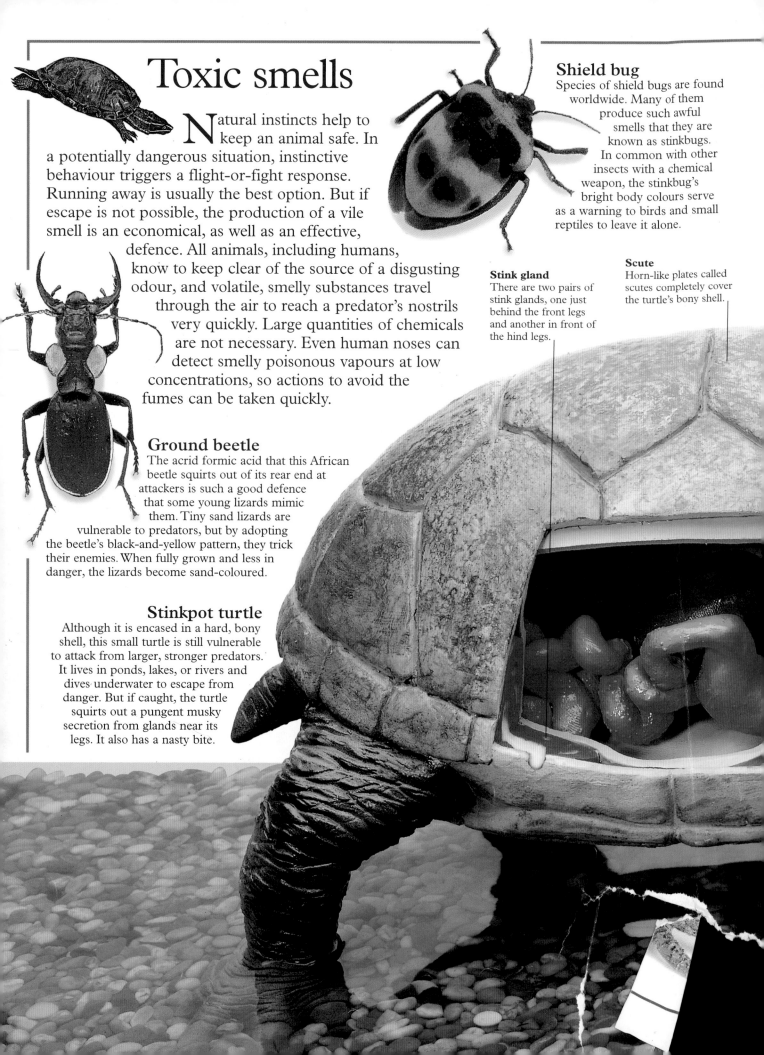

Natural instincts help to keep an animal safe. In a potentially dangerous situation, instinctive behaviour triggers a flight-or-fight response. Running away is usually the best option. But if escape is not possible, the production of a vile smell is an economical, as well as an effective, defence. All animals, including humans, know to keep clear of the source of a disgusting odour, and volatile, smelly substances travel through the air to reach a predator's nostrils very quickly. Large quantities of chemicals are not necessary. Even human noses can detect smelly poisonous vapours at low concentrations, so actions to avoid the fumes can be taken quickly.

## Shield bug
Species of shield bugs are found worldwide. Many of them produce such awful smells that they are known as stinkbugs. In common with other insects with a chemical weapon, the stinkbug's bright body colours serve as a warning to birds and small reptiles to leave it alone.

## Stink gland
There are two pairs of stink glands, one just behind the front legs and another in front of the hind legs.

## Scute
Horn-like plates called scutes completely cover the turtle's bony shell.

## Ground beetle
The acrid formic acid that this African beetle squirts out of its rear end at attackers is such a good defence that some young lizards mimic them. Tiny sand lizards are vulnerable to predators, but by adopting the beetle's black-and-yellow pattern, they trick their enemies. When fully grown and less in danger, the lizards become sand-coloured.

## Stinkpot turtle
Although it is encased in a hard, bony shell, this small turtle is still vulnerable to attack from larger, stronger predators. It lives in ponds, lakes, or rivers and dives underwater to escape from danger. But if caught, the turtle squirts out a pungent musky secretion from glands near its legs. It also has a nasty bite.

**Clever disguise**
A young caterpillar looks like a bird dropping.

## Smelly horn
A pouch behind the swallowtail caterpillar's head hides its really bizarre stink organ, the osmeterium, which shoots out whenever the caterpillar is molested. The bright-red, forked "horn" lashes about and secretes a smelly substance that is smeared onto the enemy. After use, the osmeterium is withdrawn into the pouch.

**Internal organs**
Stomach, intestine, and other organs are tightly packed inside the shell.

**Muscle**
When the turtle is picked up or threatened, muscles around the gland contract to squirt out its contents.

**Stinking froth**
The toxic foam is a good protection against hungry birds and lizards.

**Duct**
Ducts carry the smelly, yellow liquid to pores in the scutes.

**Pore**
Pores (small holes) in the scutes allow the contents of the stink gland to flow out over the surface of the shell.

## Milkweed grasshopper
The large, lazy milkweed grasshopper is reluctant to move from its food plant, the highly toxic milkweed. If the bright colours of its body and wings fail to warn off anything foolish enough to try to eat it, a mass of stinking froth pours from openings at the bases of its back legs.

**Face markings**
Two light stripes extend from the nostril to the neck.

# Stealing poison

**M**ost poisonous animals make their own venoms and poisons. For this to happen, many chemical reactions must take place, and the toxins need to be stored so that the animal is not harmed by its own poison. Like all chemical reactions, making poison uses valuable resources and energy. Some insects and other invertebrates do not make their own chemical weapons. Instead, they "steal" them from the poisonous plants or animals that make up their diet. This is an effective defence, but poses a puzzle to scientists. It is not clear how the creatures manage to avoid the poisonous effects of the toxins they eat, or how they store them in their bodies.

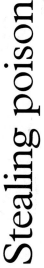

## Monarch caterpillar
Striped monarch caterpillars feed on the poisonous foliage of milkweed plants. Somehow they manage to avoid the poisonous effects of the powerful toxins in the leaves. The poison, unaltered by digestive processes, passes out of the caterpillar's gut and into its skin, making it poisonous to anything that attempts to eat it.

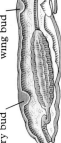

Brain

Large gut

### Hungry caterpillar
The caterpillar is primarily an eating machine. A large gut takes up most of the room inside its body. The wings and sex organs are tiny buds below the skin.

Developing wing bud

Developing ovary bud

### Pupating chrysalis
While the caterpillar pupates, dramatic changes take place. Most of its organs are replaced by adult organs. The wing and sex buds are triggered into growth.

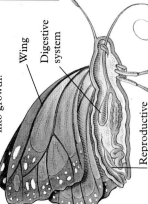

Wing

Digestive system

Reproductive system

### Emerging butterfly
Finally, an adult butterfly wriggles free of its pupal case. Blood is pumped into the crumpled wings, which expand and dry. The butterfly is ready to fly away.

## Sawfly larvae
This Australian sawfly lays batches of eggs on eucalyptus leaves, which contain high levels of a pungent oil. The young larvae huddle close together, eating the leaves. When threatened, they wave their heads about and secrete droplets of the oil from their mouths. The combined effect of these actions drives the enemy away.

**Perga larva**
The larvae resemble the caterpillars of moths and butterflies.

## Glaucus sea slug
Soft-bodied sea slugs that feed on jellyfish have evolved an ingenious way of protecting themselves. After feeding, undischarged nematocysts (p. 15) from the tentacles of its prey pass from the sea slug's gut up into hollow projections on its back. The nematocysts eventually work their way to the surface of the tissue. If the sea slug is attacked, the "stolen" nematocysts are activated and discharge their venom into the sea slug's enemy.

**Stabilising fin**
The sea slug floats on the water's surface with its tentacles outstretched.

## Monarch butterfly

The wings and skin of the monarch butterfly retain the dangerous poisons that were taken up and stored while the insect was a caterpillar. It displays striking colours and patterns on its body and wings to advertise this danger to insect-eating birds. Any that try to eat a monarch will be sick from just a taste.

**Antenna**
Long, clubbed antennae help the female locate a mate and find the right foodplants on which to lay her eggs.

**Wing**
Two pairs of conspicuously patterned wings contain poison. Just one tiny peck will warn a bird to leave the butterfly alone.

**Leg**
The first pair of legs is much too short to use for walking or balancing.

**Proboscis**
The butterfly uncoils its proboscis and uses it to draw up nectar, rather like a straw.

**Milkweed**
As an adult, the monarch feeds on milkweed nectar.

**Skin**
The butterfly's skin contains high levels of poison.

**Intestine**
A short, fairly simple intestine is all an adult butterfly needs, since it feeds on sugary nectar.

**Reproductive system**
After mating, the female butterfly lays her eggs on the young foliage of milkweed plants.

## Postman caterpillar

Brightly coloured postman butterflies live in the rainforests of South and Central America. They lay their eggs on passionflower vines. These climbers have leaves that produce cyanide-containing compounds. Postman caterpillars absorb enough of the poison to protect themselves as butterflies.

**Young leaf**
The caterpillar feeds on the youngest leaves, since they are the least poisonous.

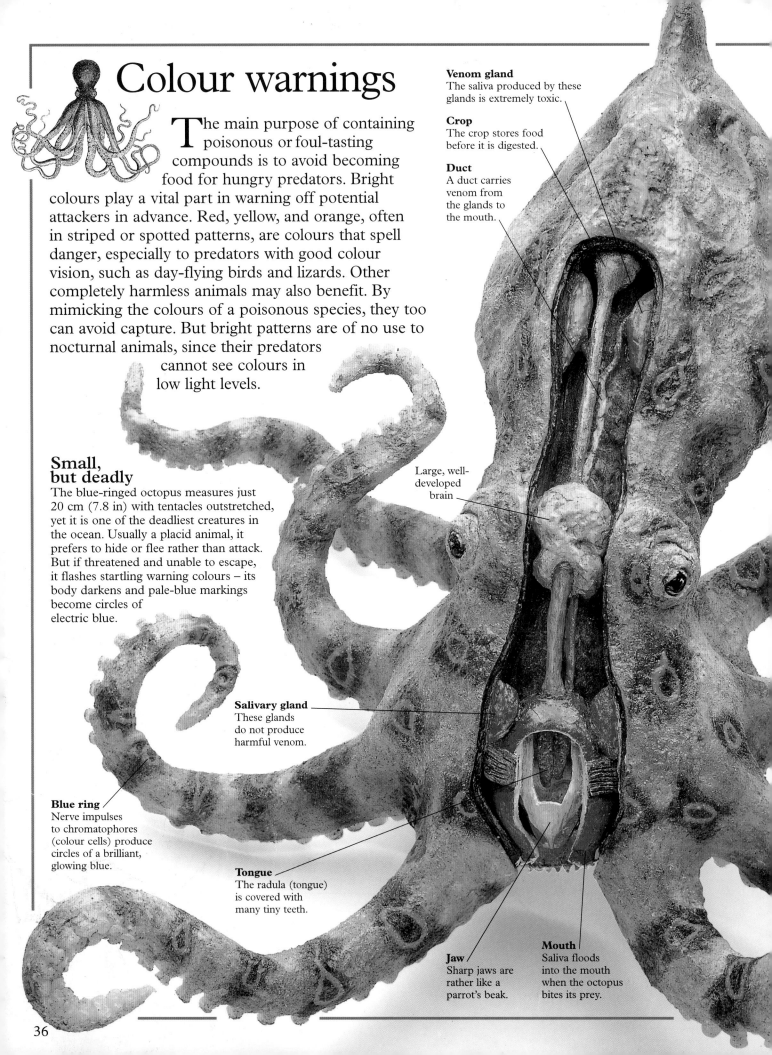

# Colour warnings

The main purpose of containing poisonous or foul-tasting compounds is to avoid becoming food for hungry predators. Bright colours play a vital part in warning off potential attackers in advance. Red, yellow, and orange, often in striped or spotted patterns, are colours that spell danger, especially to predators with good colour vision, such as day-flying birds and lizards. Other completely harmless animals may also benefit. By mimicking the colours of a poisonous species, they too can avoid capture. But bright patterns are of no use to nocturnal animals, since their predators cannot see colours in low light levels.

## Small, but deadly

The blue-ringed octopus measures just 20 cm (7.8 in) with tentacles outstretched, yet it is one of the deadliest creatures in the ocean. Usually a placid animal, it prefers to hide or flee rather than attack. But if threatened and unable to escape, it flashes startling warning colours – its body darkens and pale-blue markings become circles of electric blue.

**Venom gland**
The saliva produced by these glands is extremely toxic.

**Crop**
The crop stores food before it is digested.

**Duct**
A duct carries venom from the glands to the mouth.

Large, well-developed brain

**Salivary gland**
These glands do not produce harmful venom.

**Blue ring**
Nerve impulses to chromatophores (colour cells) produce circles of a brilliant, glowing blue.

**Tongue**
The radula (tongue) is covered with many tiny teeth.

**Jaw**
Sharp jaws are rather like a parrot's beak.

**Mouth**
Saliva floods into the mouth when the octopus bites its prey.

## Electric display

If its colour warning is ignored, the octopus injects venomous saliva into a wound that it makes with its beak-like jaws. Although the bite itself is painless and may go unnoticed, the effects of the toxic venom soon appear. Muscles are badly affected, becoming so weak that paralysis occurs and the victim has difficulty speaking and breathing. Just one octopus has enough venom to kill ten people.

**Colouring**
At night, the bright colours are not visible, so the snake loses its means of protection.

## Sinaloan milk snake

This milk snake is harmless, but its bright red, black, and yellow pattern makes it look very similar to a coral snake, which is venomous. By mimicking the colouring of a dangerous species, the snake protects itself from predators.

**Bands**
Patterns signal a warning to predators.

**False eyes**
In its threat position, these spots look like the eyes of a snake.

## Caterpillar or snake?

The caterpillar of the elephant hawkmoth is large and succulent, making it a tasty mouthful for a bird, but it has a clever way of protecting itself. The caterpillar has eyespots at the front of its body. When alarmed, it puffs up its throat and displays these false eyes, giving the impression that the caterpillar is a venomous snake.

**Red for danger**
Blotchy, red belly warns that the toad tastes awful.

**Staying hidden**
Mottled brown or green body is an effective camouflage.

## Fire-bellied toad

Seen from above, the fire-bellied toad is mottled brown or green. If disturbed by a large, hungry predator, it rears up or hollows its back and twists its legs round, exposing its bright-red or yellow underside.

**Tentacle**
The tentacles lined with suckers are quite harmless to humans.

## Harlequin bug

This brightly coloured shield bug from Australia has a dreadful taste that protects it from birds and other predators. The female lays neat batches of eggs around the stems of eucalyptus leaves. She guards these eggs until they hatch, using her vivid colouring to protect the developing young.

# Nasty mouthfuls

The poison of some creatures is present only in their skin or flesh, so they are not harmful unless they are eaten. This is not very effective as a defence, because by the time the predator realises that it has a poisonous meal, it is too late. The toxic victim will be dead, possibly completely consumed. If it is not killed by the poison, a carnivore that has suffered ill effects from eating a nasty mouthful will make sure it does not happen again, and stay well clear in future. This protects the species, but not the individual. It is much more useful if an animal with poisonous flesh has a brightly coloured or patterned body to warn off potential predators in advance.

**Body colouring**
The patchy colours of the slow-swiming puffer help it merge with dappled light shining from above.

**Insectivore**
The shrew feeds mainly on insects.

**Teeth**
A puffer has four sharp teeth, which it uses to crunch through shellfish.

**Pharynx**
Muscles in the wall of the pharynx contract to draw water in and force it into the stomach.

## Puffer fish
Many species of puffer fish are deadly poisonous. Their powerful toxin lies chiefly in the ovaries, liver, and intestine. Since puffer flesh is a highly prized delicacy in Japan, specially trained, licensed chefs meticulously remove all traces of the poisonous tissues before serving it. Even so, there are still several deaths every year in Japan from eating puffers.

## Water shrew
Many shrews have venomous saliva, and glands along their sides that exude distasteful chemicals. Some predators, such as owls, are not deterred by these noxious secretions. Others find them repellent and leave these shrews alone.

**Uninflated puffer**
Uninflated, the puffer looks like any typical fish.

**Stomach**
Water inflates the stomach to many times its usual size.

## Puffing a puffer
When it is alarmed or threatened, the puffer starts to gulp down water. This causes the stomach to swell and the whole body to become almost spherical, making it harder for attackers to swallow.

**Skin**
The skin covering the expanded stomach stretches out thinly.

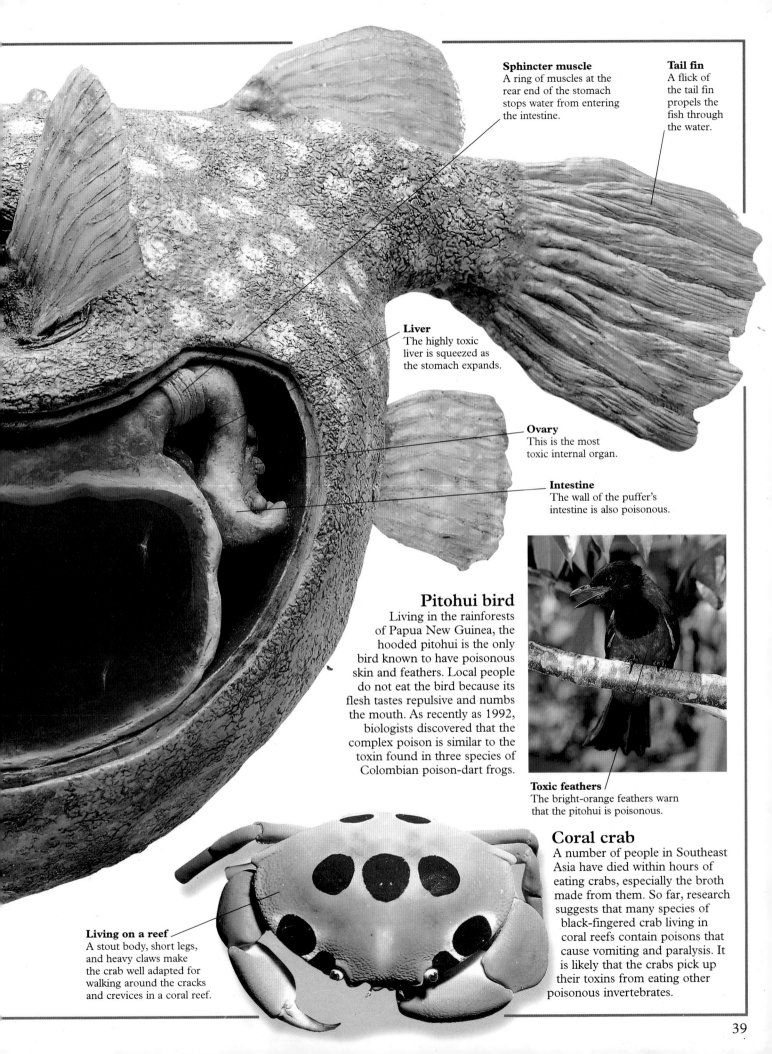

**Sphincter muscle**
A ring of muscles at the rear end of the stomach stops water from entering the intestine.

**Tail fin**
A flick of the tail fin propels the fish through the water.

**Liver**
The highly toxic liver is squeezed as the stomach expands.

**Ovary**
This is the most toxic internal organ.

**Intestine**
The wall of the puffer's intestine is also poisonous.

## Pitohui bird
Living in the rainforests of Papua New Guinea, the hooded pitohui is the only bird known to have poisonous skin and feathers. Local people do not eat the bird because its flesh tastes repulsive and numbs the mouth. As recently as 1992, biologists discovered that the complex poison is similar to the toxin found in three species of Colombian poison-dart frogs.

**Toxic feathers**
The bright-orange feathers warn that the pitohui is poisonous.

## Coral crab
A number of people in Southeast Asia have died within hours of eating crabs, especially the broth made from them. So far, research suggests that many species of black-fingered crab living in coral reefs contain poisons that cause vomiting and paralysis. It is likely that the crabs pick up their toxins from eating other poisonous invertebrates.

**Living on a reef**
A stout body, short legs, and heavy claws make the crab well adapted for walking around the cracks and crevices in a coral reef.

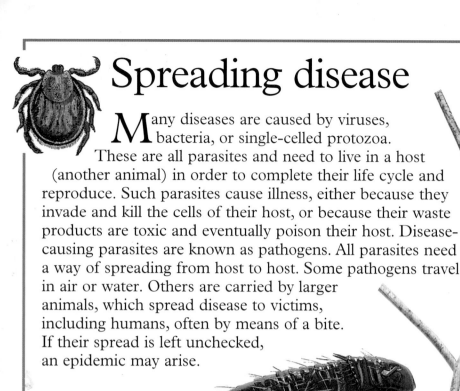

# Spreading disease

Many diseases are caused by viruses, bacteria, or single-celled protozoa. These are all parasites and need to live in a host (another animal) in order to complete their life cycle and reproduce. Such parasites cause illness, either because they invade and kill the cells of their host, or because their waste products are toxic and eventually poison their host. Disease-causing parasites are known as pathogens. All parasites need a way of spreading from host to host. Some pathogens travel in air or water. Others are carried by larger animals, which spread disease to victims, including humans, often by means of a bite. If their spread is left unchecked, an epidemic may arise.

**Colour change**
As it swells with blood, the tick changes colour from yellow to dark red.

**Human hair**
Ticks feed on humans only if they are really hungry.

**Jumping flea**
A flea can jump up to 100 times its body length.

## Cat flea
Mammals that return regularly to the same nest or bed often have fleas. The eggs and larvae thrive in warm, damp nests, and even adult fleas do not need to spend all their time on their host. Cat fleas spread tapeworms and roundworms from cat to cat. The bubonic plague, a deadly disease, is caused by a bacterium spread by some rat fleas.

**Swollen body**
A well-fed tick is roughly the size of a small bean.

**Feeler**
Sensitive feelers help position the mouthparts in the victim's skin.

**Blood sucker**
As the mosquito sucks up blood, it injects *Plasmodium* along with its saliva.

## Paralysis tick
All ticks feed on the blood of animals and people, and many carry bacteria that cause disease. The Australian paralysis tick has toxic saliva that can cause paralysis, or in some cases death, if it is not removed in time. The tick prefers to cling to a furry host. When it sticks to humans, it is commonly found under hair at the back of the neck.

## Malaria mosquito
Malaria is caused by *Plasmodium*, a single-celled organism that multiplies in red blood cells. Bouts of fever occur when these blood cells burst, releasing more *Plasmodium* and waste products. Only the female mosquito spreads the disease. If it sucks blood from a malaria carrier, the next person it feeds on will become infected.

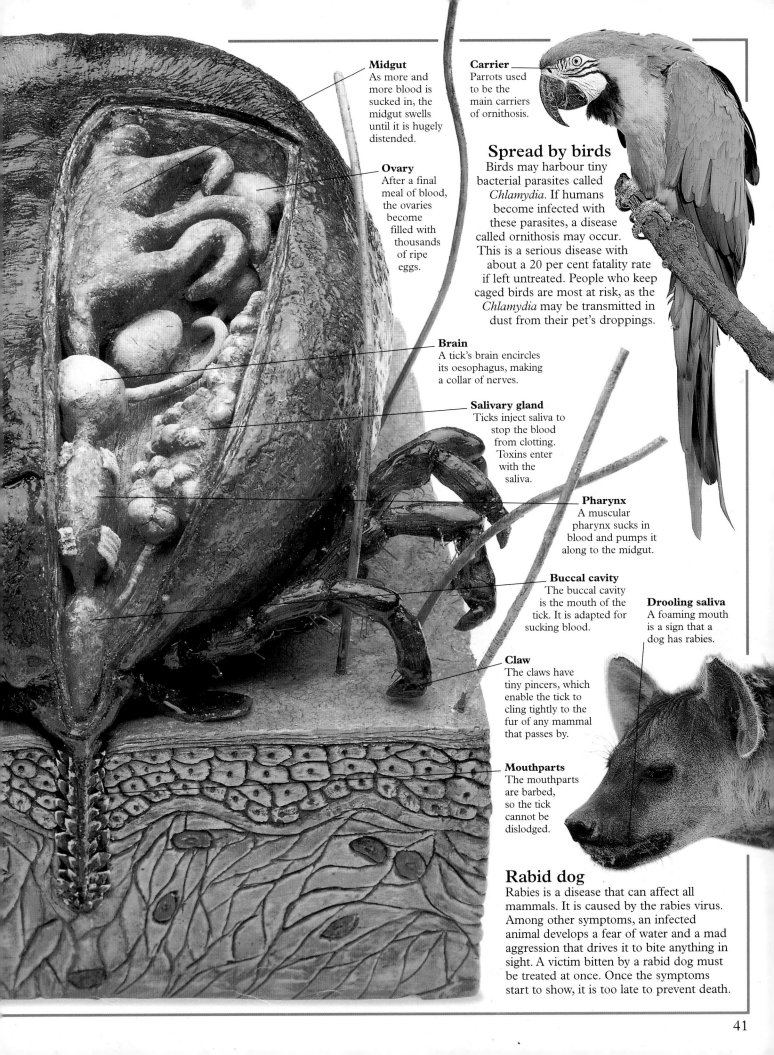

**Midgut**
As more and more blood is sucked in, the midgut swells until it is hugely distended.

**Ovary**
After a final meal of blood, the ovaries become filled with thousands of ripe eggs.

**Carrier**
Parrots used to be the main carriers of ornithosis.

## Spread by birds
Birds may harbour tiny bacterial parasites called *Chlamydia*. If humans become infected with these parasites, a disease called ornithosis may occur. This is a serious disease with about a 20 per cent fatality rate if left untreated. People who keep caged birds are most at risk, as the *Chlamydia* may be transmitted in dust from their pet's droppings.

**Brain**
A tick's brain encircles its oesophagus, making a collar of nerves.

**Salivary gland**
Ticks inject saliva to stop the blood from clotting. Toxins enter with the saliva.

**Pharynx**
A muscular pharynx sucks in blood and pumps it along to the midgut.

**Buccal cavity**
The buccal cavity is the mouth of the tick. It is adapted for sucking blood.

**Drooling saliva**
A foaming mouth is a sign that a dog has rabies.

**Claw**
The claws have tiny pincers, which enable the tick to cling tightly to the fur of any mammal that passes by.

**Mouthparts**
The mouthparts are barbed, so the tick cannot be dislodged.

## Rabid dog
Rabies is a disease that can affect all mammals. It is caused by the rabies virus. Among other symptoms, an infected animal develops a fear of water and a mad aggression that drives it to bite anything in sight. A victim bitten by a rabid dog must be treated at once. Once the symptoms start to show, it is too late to prevent death.

# Glossary

Timber rattlesnake with its fangs folded away

## A

### Abdomen
The part of an animal's body that contains most of the digestive, reproductive, and excretory organs.

### Allergy
A violent reaction by the body's immune system to chemicals that cause mild symptoms, if any, in most people.

### Amphibian
An animal, such as a frog, toad, or salamander, that can live on land, but must return to water to breed.

### Antivenin
Blood serum containing antibodies, which work against the toxic components of some venoms.

## B

### Bacterium
A very small, simple, single-celled organism. Many bacteria cause disease.

## C

### Chrysalis
The pupating stage of a butterfly or moth, in which it turns from a caterpillar to a flying adult.

### Claws
Sharp, horny nails on the tips of an animal's toes, which are used to dig or climb.

Giant tiger centipede

## D

### Dermis
The lower layer of skin, which lies beneath the epidermis. It contains hair follicles, blood vessels, and nerve endings.

## E

### Enzyme
A substance that causes vital chemical reactions to take place, but which is not used up itself in the process.

### Epidemic
An outbreak of the same disease among a large number of people at the same time.

### Epidermis
The outer, protective layer of skin. It covers the inner layer, or dermis.

## F

### Fangs
Long, sharp teeth that can pierce another animal's flesh and through which venom can be injected.

## H

### Haemotoxin
A poisonous substance that affects the blood.

### Histamine
A chemical that often provokes an allergic reaction in sensitive individuals.

## I

### Invertebrate
An animal, such as an insect, spider, jellyfish, or centipede, that does not have a backbone.

## M

### Mammal
A warm-blooded animal, such as a water shrew or duck-billed platypus, that is covered in fur or hair and suckles its young on milk.

### Mandibles
Another name for the jaws of insects, spiders, crabs, centipedes, and other invertebrates that have a jointed outer body layer.

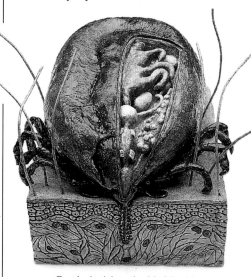

Paralysis tick embedded in skin

## N

### Nematocyst
A minute capsule in some cells of jellyfish, anemones, and corals. When triggered, the nematocyst shoots out a venom-injecting thread into the flesh of prey or enemies.

### Neurotoxin
A poisonous substance that affects the nervous system.

## O

### Oesophagus
The tube that carries chewed food from the throat-like pharynx to the stomach.

### Ovary
The part of the female reproductive system in which the egg cells are produced and nourished.

# P

## Paralyse

To affect the way nerves work to such an extent that movement, sometimes including breathing and heart function, becomes impossible.

## Parasite

An organism that is dependent upon a living animal of another species for all its nourishment. It cannot live apart from its host.

## Pathogen

An organism or other agent that causes another organism to develop a disease.

## Pedipalps

A short pair of feelers on a spider's head. Male spiders have pedipalps that are modified to transfer sperm to the female during mating.

## Pharynx

The part of the digestive system that lies behind the mouth and just in front of the oesophagus.

## Pincers

The enlarged claws of animals, such as scorpions and crabs, that grip together in a pinching action.

## Poison

A harmful chemical present in some animals, whose effects are felt only after it has been inhaled or swallowed.

## Predator

A carnivorous (flesh-eating) animal that actively hunts and kills its prey in order to survive.

Funnel-web spider rearing up in a strike position

## Proboscis

The coiled, tube-like mouthparts of a butterfly or moth. It can uncoil to suck up liquids.

## Pupate

To undergo the complete internal and external reorganisation that changes a caterpillar into a butterfly or moth.

# R

## Reptile

A cold-blooded animal, often with scaly skin. A reptile may either lay eggs or give birth to live young.

# S

## Saliva

Liquid in the mouth that moistens the food and begins the process of digestion.

## Secretion

A substance, such as saliva or skin poison, that is produced inside cells, but which passes out of the cell to carry out its function.

## Species

A group of organisms with similar features, which reproduce with each other.

## Spider

An invertebrate with a head and thorax combined into a cephalothorax, and eight legs.

Inflated puffer fish

## Sting

A slender, needle-like organ that can penetrate another animal's skin to inject a dose of venom.

# T

## Tentacles

Long, flexible arm-like structures that can be used for grasping or moving, as well as for feeling.

## Tetrodotoxin

A lethal toxin found in the skin and some internal organs of puffer fish. It causes paralysis and death.

## Trachea

A tube in the throat of a reptile, bird, or mammal that carries air towards the lungs.

## Tubercle

The name given to tiny lumps on the surface of the skin of some creatures, such as caterpillars or toads.

# V

## Venom

A mixture of harmful chemicals that one animal may inject into another animal by means of fangs, hairs, spines, or stings.

## Vertebrate

An animal, such as a frog, lizard, bird, or mammal, that has a backbone.

## Virus

A microscopic organism that can multiply only when inside the cells of a host. Many viruses cause disease.

# Index

# Acknowledgements

**Thanks to:** Paul Hillyard and Martin Brendell at the Natural History Museum, London for advice; Robert Graham for research; Dave Morgan for photographic assistance; Marion Dent for the index.

**Visualization of book:** Dominic Zwemmer

**Editorial and design assistance:** Goldberry Broad, Nancy Jones, Jayne Parsons, and Jake Williamson

**Illustrations:** Patrizia Donaera 9; John Woodcock 10; 12; 14; 17; 19; 24; 34

**Additional photography:** Andy Crawford, Jerry Young

**Picture Credits:**
The publisher would like to thank the following for their kind permission to reproduce their photographs:

**Key:** c=centre; b=bottom; t=top; l=left; r=right; a=above

**Ardea:** Pascal Goetgheluck 40bl
**Auscape:** Kathie Atkinson 18c; John Cancalosi 11tl; Andy Purcell 28bl; C. Andrew Henley 24cl; Becca Saunders 18bl; Jany Sauvanet 9bc
**Bruce Coleman:** Adrian Davies 29b; Joe McDonald 29br; Andy Purcell 28bl; Dr Frieder Sauer 27bc **Michael and Patricia Fogden:** Michael Fogden 12bc **Minden Pictures:** Mark Moffett 16bl; **Nature Focus:** P.G. Roach 11bl; **NHPA:** ANT 20bl; Anthony Bannister 26bl, 29tr; Nigel J. Dennis 41br; Daniel Heuclin 17bl, 39cr; Michael Tweedie 12tr **Natural Science Photos:** M. Andera 38cl; I. Bennett 34bc; Dave B. Fleetham 20bc; Andrew Watts 37cra

**Oxford Scientific Films:** Scott Camazine 14bl; Scott Camazine/K. Visscher 13c; Densey Clyne/Mantis Wildlife Films 22cl below; Pam/Willy Kemp 21bl; Renee Lynn 27cl below; Tom McHugh 24bc; K.G. Vock/Okapia endpapers **Planet Earth Pictures:** Gary Bell 10tr, 19tr; Georgette Douwma 21br; Nick Garbutt 30cl; Roger de la Harpe 10bl; Ken Lucas 30bl; David Maitland 37br; Paulo de Oliveira 22c; Linda Pitkin 39bc **Premaphotos Wildlife:** K.G. Preston-Mafham 24tr, 33tr, 34cl